CELEBRATE!

Betty Crocker CELEBRATE!

A Year-Round Guide
to Holiday Food and Fun

WILEY

Wiley Publishing, Inc.

Published by Wiley Publishing, Inc., Hoboken, NJ

Library of Congress Cataloging-in-Publication Data:

Crocker, Betty.
  Betty Crocker celebrate! : a year-round guide to holiday food and fun.— 1st ed.
    p. cm.
  Includes bibliographical references and index.
  ISBN 0-7645-6848-5
  1. Holiday cookery. I. Title: Holiday cookbook. II. Title.
  TX739.C73 2004
  641.5'68—dc22   2004002291

Manufactured in the United States of America

10 9 8 7 6 5 4 3 2

Cover photos, clockwise: Fruit Kabobs with Tropical Fruit Coulis (page 220), "Cran-tinis" (page 163), Strawberry Santas (page 226), Honey Lime Fruit Salad (page 118)

GENERAL MILLS, INC.

Director, Book and Online Publishing: Kim Walter

Manager, Book Publishing: Lois L. Tlusty

Editor: Lois L. Tlusty

Recipe Development and Testing: Betty Crocker Kitchens

Food Stylists: Betty Crocker Kitchens

Photography: General Mills Photo Studios

WILEY PUBLISHING, INC.

Publisher: Natalie Chapman

Executive Editor: Anne Ficklen

Assistant Editor: Pamela Adler

Senior Production Editor: Jennifer Mazurkie

Cover design: Paul Dinovo

Book design: Vertigo Design NYC

Interior Layout: Holly Wittenberg

Manufacturing Buyer: Kevin Watt

The Betty Crocker Kitchens seal guarantees success in your kitchen. Every recipe has been tested in America's Most Trusted Kitchens™ to meet our high standards of reliability, easy preparation and great taste.

FOR MORE GREAT IDEAS VISIT *BettyCrocker*.com

Dear Friends,

Get ready to celebrate! Everybody loves holidays, from big festive gatherings to small and intimate parties. That's why you'll find seventeen favorite holidays in this one handy book—so you can party all year 'round! Start with a New Year's Eve Dinner that rings in a full year of merriment and fun, a year of enjoying the "big" holidays— Halloween, Thanksgiving, Hanukkah, Christmas, as well as ones that may be new to you, such as Chinese New Year, Cinco de Mayo and Kwanzaa.

Don't forget those holidays that are familiar but for which there often is no game plan—Memorial Day, Independence Day or Labor Day. With these easy menus and decorating ideas, it's a cinch to invite the gang over and still enjoy the holiday.

Feeling a little sentimental? You'll definitely want to check out ideas for Valentine's Day, Mother's Day and Father's Day. Make these days truly special with great menus and easy crafts that tell the special people in your life just how important they are.

And, of course, there are holidays with a religious history—Passover, Easter, St. Patrick's Day. So many of us like to acknowledge a variety of religious holidays (including Christmas and Hanukkah) and you'll find great ideas here, especially helpful if you're hosting a holiday for the first time.

Whatever you want to celebrate—here's a no-fail plan for you! Easy menus, beautiful photos, inventive craft ideas and holiday history give fresh and welcome ideas for both the classic holidays, and "new" holidays. So, turn the page and get ready for fun!

Warmly,

Betty Crocker

CELEBRATE!

CONTENTS

NEW YEAR'S EVE

JANUARY GET ITS NAME FROM JANUS, a Roman god who was always pictured with two faces: one glancing back at the past and one looking ahead to the future. Many of us begin the month in a similar way—reminiscing about events of the previous year, while eagerly looking forward to what's to come. The first of January often inspires people to make a fresh start, and you know what that means: New Year's resolutions. If one of your resolutions is to spend more time with family and friends, try ringing in the new year with a festive, low-key buffet. This serve-yourself meal, which goes perfectly with champagne, will keep everyone well fed while they wait for the clock to strike midnight. And if the kids manage to stay awake, let them in on the celebration with sparkling grape juice and truffles!

MIDNIGHT BUFFET

SERVES 12

*Pesto Salmon Roulades

*Double-Cheese Fondue

*Fresh Basil-Wrapped Cheese Balls

*Gingered Fruit Salsa with Crispy Cinnamon Chips

*Cranberry Chicken Salad Tarts

*Cinnamon Truffles

Champagne and Sparkling Grape Juice

* RECIPE FOLLOWS

Pesto Salmon Roulades

PREP: 15 MINUTES • 28 APPETIZERS

1 package (6 ounces) salmon lox

1/3 cup basil pesto

1/2 cup drained roasted red bell peppers
(from 7-ounce jar), cut into thin strips

28 roasted-garlic bagel chips

1. Cut each salmon piece lengthwise in half so that it is about 3/4 inch wide. Spread each with about 1/2 teaspoon of the pesto; top with roasted bell pepper strip. Carefully roll up.

2. Place each roulade on a bagel chip. Serve immediately.

one appetizer: Calories 65 (Calories from Fat 25); Fat 3g; (Saturated 1g); Cholesterol 0mg; Sodium 125mg; Carbohydrate 7g (Dietary Fiber 0g); Protein 2g. % Daily Value: Vitamin A 4%; Vitamin C 4%; Calcium 2%; Iron 2%. Diet Exchanges: 1/2 Starch, 1/2 Fat. Carbohydrate Choices: 1/2

holiday FLAVOR *twist*

Look for other flavors of bagel chips besides garlic. Good choices include rosemary-garlic, ranch and sea salt bagel chips.

Double-Cheese Fondue

PREP: 15 MINUTES • COOK: 15 MINUTES • 20 SERVINGS (2 TABLESPOONS EACH)

1 1/2 cups shredded Havarti cheese (6 ounces)

1 cup shredded sharp Cheddar cheese (4 ounces)

2 tablespoons all-purpose flour

1/2 cup chicken broth

1/3 cup milk

1/2 cup sliced sun-dried tomatoes in oil, drained

4 medium green onions, sliced (1/4 cup)

Crisp breadsticks, if desired

Cut-up fresh vegetables, if desired

holiday tip
DO-AHEAD

Fondue is a great dish to take to someone's home during the holidays. Just make it ahead, pack it in a resealable container and take it, along with your fondue pot. Once you arrive, pour the fondue into the pot and turn it on warm/simmer setting.

1. Place cheeses and flour in a resealable plastic food-storage bag. Shake until cheese is coated with flour. Heat broth and milk in fondue pot just to a simmer over warm/simmer setting.

2. Add cheese mixture, about 1 cup at a time, stirring with wire whisk until melted. Cook over warm/simmer setting, stirring constantly, until slightly thickened. Stir in tomatoes and onions.

3. Keep warm over warm/simmer setting. Serve with breadsticks and vegetables.

one serving: Calories 80 (Calories from Fat 55); Fat 6g; (Saturated 3g); Cholesterol 15mg; Sodium 185mg; Carbohydrate 2g (Dietary Fiber 0g); Protein 4g. % Daily Value: Vitamin A 4%; Vitamin C 2%; Calcium 8%; Iron 0%. Diet Exchanges: 1/2 High-Fat Meat. Carbohydrate Choices: 0

Fresh Basil-Wrapped Cheese Balls

PREP: 15 MINUTES • CHILL: 30 MINUTES • 24 APPETIZERS

1/2 cup mascarpone cheese (4 ounces)

1/2 cup crumbled Gorgonzola cheese (2 ounces)

2 tablespoons grated Parmesan cheese

1/8 teaspoon pepper

24 fresh basil leaves, 2 to 2 1/2 inches long

holiday
FLAVOR *twist*

If mascarpone isn't available, you can still make these tasty holiday treats. Use a 3-ounce package of cream cheese, softened.

1. Mix cheeses and pepper until blended. Cover and refrigerate about 30 minutes or until firm enough to shape into balls.

2. Shape 1 1/2 teaspoons cheese mixture into a ball. Roll slightly to form an oval, about 1 inch long. Place on wide end of basil leaf; roll up. Roll leaf and cheese between fingers to form an oval. Repeat with remaining cheese mixture and basil leaves.

3. Serve immediately, or cover with plastic wrap and refrigerate until serving but no longer than 2 hours.

one appetizer: Calories 25 (Calories from Fat 25); Fat 3g; (Saturated 2g); Cholesterol 5mg; Sodium 55mg; Carbohydrate 0g (Dietary Fiber 0g); Protein 1g. % Daily Value: Vitamin A 2%; Vitamin C 0%; Calcium 2%; Iron 0%. Diet Exchanges: 1/2 Fat. Carbohydrate Choices: 0

Gingered Fruit Salsa
with Crispy Cinnamon Chips

PREP: 30 MINUTES • BROIL: 8 MINUTES • 24 SERVINGS (2 TABLESPOONS SALSA AND 3 CHIPS EACH)

1 tablespoon sugar

2 teaspoons ground cinnamon

6 flour tortillas (8 to 10 inches in diameter)

3 tablespoons butter or margarine, melted

1 cup finely diced pineapple

1 cup finely diced papaya

1 cup finely diced mango

1/4 cup chopped fresh cilantro

1 tablespoon finely chopped crystallized ginger

1 tablespoon lemon juice

1/8 teaspoon salt

1. Set oven control to broil. Mix sugar and cinnamon. Brush both sides of each tortilla with butter; sprinkle with sugar-cinnamon mixture. Cut each tortilla into 12 wedges.

2. Place tortilla wedges in single layer in 2 ungreased jelly roll pans, 15 1/2 × 10 1/2 × 1 inch, or on 2 cookie sheets. Broil 2 to 4 minutes, turning once, until crispy and golden brown. Cool completely.

3. Mix remaining ingredients. Serve salsa with chips.

one serving: Calories 60 (Calories from Fat 20); Fat 2g; (Saturated 1g); Cholesterol 5mg; Sodium 75mg; Carbohydrate 10g (Dietary Fiber 1g); Protein 1g. % Daily Value: Vitamin A 4%; Vitamin C 14%; Calcium 2%; Iron 2%. Diet Exchanges: 1/2 Fruit, 1/2 Fat. Carbohydrate Choices: 1/2

holiday FLAVOR *twist*

Use 3 cups finely chopped pineapple if the fresh papaya and mango aren't available. Your buffet will be just as tasty and colorful.

holiday DO-AHEAD *tip*

Save time the day of your New Year's buffet by making the chips up to 1 week ahead. Just store them in a tightly covered container at room temperature.

Cranberry Chicken Salad Tarts

PREP: 15 MINUTES • 15 TARTS

1 package (2.1 ounces) frozen mini fillo dough shells

1/2 cup deli chicken salad spread

2 tablespoons dried cranberries

1/2 teaspoon chopped fresh or 1/8 teaspoon dried marjoram leaves

1 to 2 tablespoons chopped pistachio nuts

15 small sprigs marjoram

holiday
DO-AHEAD *tip*

You can assemble these appetizers and keep them refrigerated for up to 2 hours before serving. Relax and enjoy the party!

1. Let package of frozen fillo shells stand at room temperature 10 minutes.

2. Mix chicken salad spread, cranberries and chopped marjoram. Spoon heaping teaspoonful mixture into each fillo shell.

3. Sprinkle with nuts. Garnish each with marjoram sprig.

one tart: Calories 30 (Calories from Fat 10); Fat 1g; (Saturated 0g); Cholesterol 5mg; Sodium 30mg; Carbohydrate 4g (Dietary Fiber 1g); Protein 1g. % Daily Value: Vitamin A 0%; Vitamin C 0%; Calcium 0%; Iron 0%. Diet Exchanges: 1/2 Other Carbohydrates. Carbohydrate Choices: 0

Cinnamon Truffles

PREP: 35 MINUTES • COOK: 5 MINUTES • CHILL: 2 HOURS • STAND: 30 MINUTES • ABOUT 24 TRUFFLES

1 bag (12 ounces) semisweet chocolate chips (2 cups)

1 tablespoon butter or margarine

1/4 cup whipping (heavy) cream

1 teaspoon vanilla

1/2 teaspoon ground cinnamon

Powdered sugar, if desired

Baking cocoa, if desired

holiday tip
DO-AHEAD

Prepare these decadent truffles at least one day ahead. Like the photo? To serve truffles like this, punch small hole in bottom of silver paper candy cups. Insert an 8- to 12-inch lollipop stick through bottom of a cup and then into a truffle. Wrap thin ribbon around the stick. Place truffle "pops" in a simple silver cup or pitcher.

1. Line cookie sheet with aluminum foil or parchment paper. Melt chocolate chips and butter in heavy 2-quart saucepan over low heat, stirring constantly; remove from heat.

2. Stir in whipping cream, vanilla and cinnamon. Refrigerate 30 to 60 minutes, stirring frequently, just until firm enough to roll into balls.

3. Drop mixture by tablespoonfuls onto cookie sheet. Shape into balls. (If mixture is too sticky, refrigerate until firm enough to shape.) Refrigerate about 1 hour until firm.

4. Sprinkle half of the truffles with powdered sugar and half with cocoa. Store in airtight container in refrigerator for up to 1 week. Remove truffles from refrigerator about 30 minutes before serving; serve at room temperature.

one truffle: Calories 90 (Calories from Fat 55); Fat 6g; (Saturated 3g); Cholesterol 5mg; Sodium 5mg; Carbohydrate 9g (Dietary Fiber 1g); Protein 1g. % Daily Value: Vitamin A 0%; Vitamin C 0%; Calcium 0%; Iron 2%. Diet Exchanges: 1/2 Starch, 1 Fat. Carbohydrate Choices: 1/2

Champagne Cookies

What a surprise when you "pop the cork" on these cookies! They'll be the hit of any New Year's eve gathering.

WHAT YOU NEED:

Nontoxic glue

Lightweight cardboard

Favorite recipe for sugar cookies (page 210) or purchased dough

Royal Icing (below) or other powdered sugar glaze

Green paste food coloring

Candy decorations

Shredded paper

Long, rectangular box

HOW TO DO IT:

1. Enlarge pictures of a bottle and champagne glass from a magazine to life-size, using a photocopier. Glue copies of bottle and glass on cardboard. Cut around shapes to use as a pattern for cookies.

2. Prepare cookie dough. Roll about 1/4 inch thick on floured cookie sheet. Freeze 3 to 5 minutes to harden dough. Place cardboard shapes on dough. Cut around shapes, using paring knife; remove extra dough from around shapes. Bake as directed in cookie recipe; cool.

3. Prepare Royal Icing. Divide icing in half. Tint half of icing green, using food coloring. Spoon into decorating bag with plain tip or spoon into a resealable plastic bag and cut off small corner for writing tip. Pipe icing onto cookies. Add candy decorations.

4. Place shredded paper in box; add cookies. Cover with plastic wrap if desired.

Royal Icing

Beat 4 cups powdered sugar, 3 tablespoons meringue powder and 6 to 8 tablespoons warm water in large bowl with electric mixer on high speed until smooth and fluffy. If icing is too thin, beat in additional powdered sugar, 1 tablespoon at a time. Cover until ready to use.

Betty Crocker.com

CHINESE NEW YEAR

THE FIRST NEW MOON of the new year marks the start of the Chinese New Year, and the full moon signals the end of the 15-day celebration. The festive holiday is filled with family reunions, lavish meals and ceremonies to honor ancestors who have passed away. Future prosperity is a common theme and children are often given red envelopes with coins inside for luck. No sweeping or dusting is done on the first day of the year for fear that good fortune will be swept out the door. So, why not start the season as the Chinese do and open all the doors and windows in your home at midnight to usher out the old year and welcome in the new year?

CHINESE NEW YEAR DINNER

SERVES 6

*Spicy Chicken Wings

*Stir-fried Red Snapper

*Stir-fried Noodles with Vegetables

*Pork Fried Rice

or

White Rice

*Gingered Pineapple

Coconut Ice Cream or Lime Sorbet

*RECIPE FOLLOWS

Fun with the Zodiac

Check out your birthday—are you a friendly horse or maybe a hard-working rooster? Have fun looking up everyone's signs and comparing character traits!

Chinese Animal Zodiac

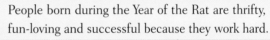

1932, 1944, 1956, 1968, 1980, 1992, 2004 — People born during the Year of the Monkey are clever and have a lot of common sense.

1933, 1945, 1957, 1969, 1981, 1993, 2005 — People born during the Year of the Rooster are deep-thinkers and hard workers.

1934, 1946, 1958, 1970, 1982, 1994, 2006 — People born during the Year of the Dog are honest, very loyal and committed to justice for everyone.

1935, 1947, 1959, 1971, 1983, 1995, 2007 — People born during the Year of the Boar are courageous, tenacious and eager to learn new things.

1936, 1948, 1960, 1972, 1984, 1996, 2008 — People born during the Year of the Rat are thrifty, fun-loving and successful because they work hard.

1937, 1949, 1961, 1973, 1985, 1997, 2009 — People born during the Year of the Ox are patient and quiet but often stubborn.

1938, 1950, 1962, 1974, 1986, 1998, 2010 — People born during the Year of the Tiger are deep-thinkers who quickly go to the aid of their friends.

1939, 1951, 1963, 1975, 1987, 1999, 2011 — People born during the Year of the Rabbit are lucky, very talented and financially successful.

1940, 1952, 1964, 1976, 1988, 2000, 2012 — People born during the Year of the Dragon are honest, trustworthy, healthy and full of energy.

1941, 1953, 1965, 1977, 1989, 2001, 2013 — People born during the Year of the Snake are wise and succeed in almost everything they do.

1942, 1954, 1966, 1978, 1990, 2002, 2014 — People born during the Year of the Horse are very smart, extremely friendly and like to talk.

1943, 1955, 1967, 1979, 1991, 2003, 2015 — People born during the Year of the Ram are artistic, gentle and compassionate.

Spicy Chicken Wings

PREP: 25 MINUTES • CHILL: 1 HOUR • BAKE: 50 MINUTES • 40 APPETIZERS

20 chicken wings (about 4 pounds)

1/4 cup dry sherry or chicken broth

1/4 cup oyster sauce

1/4 cup honey

3 tablespoons chopped fresh cilantro

2 tablespoons chili sauce

2 tablespoons grated lime peel

4 medium green onions, chopped (1/4 cup)

3 cloves garlic, finely chopped

holiday shortcut

Want to wing this recipe? Then buy chicken drummettes (you will need about 40) instead of chicken wings. Drummettes are already cut-up and ready for marinating, so you'll save some time in the prep.

holiday tip
DO-AHEAD

You can prepare and bake these zesty wings up to 24 hours ahead. Cover with aluminum foil and refrigerate. To reheat, place the covered pan in the oven at 350° for 20 to 25 minutes or until chicken is heated through.

1. Cut each chicken wing at joints to make 3 pieces; discard tip. Cut off and discard excess skin.

2. Mix remaining ingredients in resealable heavy-duty plastic food-storage bag or large glass bowl. Add chicken to marinade. Seal bag; turn to coat. Refrigerate at least 1 hour but no longer than 24 hours, turning once.

3. Heat oven to 375°. Place chicken in ungreased jelly roll pan, 15 1/2 × 10 1/2 × 1 inch. Bake uncovered 30 minutes, stirring frequently. Bake about 20 minutes longer or until juice of chicken is no longer pink when centers of thickest pieces are cut.

one appetizer: Calories 60 (Calories from Fat 25); Fat 3g; (Saturated 1g); Cholesterol 15mg; Sodium 75mg; Carbohydrate 3g (Dietary Fiber 0g); Protein 5g. % Daily Value: Vitamin A 0%; Vitamin C 0%; Calcium 0%; Iron 0%. Diet Exchanges: 1/2 High-Fat Meat. Carbohydrate Choices: 0

Stir-Fried Red Snapper

PREP: 15 MINUTES • COOK: 15 MINUTES • 6 SERVINGS

1 1/4 pounds red snapper or other lean fish fillets, about 1 inch thick

2 teaspoons teriyaki marinade and sauce

2 teaspoons cornstarch

1 tablespoon vegetable oil

2 medium tomatoes, coarsely chopped

1 medium onion, coarsely chopped

1 clove garlic, crushed

1/4 cup teriyaki marinade and sauce

1/4 cup dry white wine or apple juice

1/2 teaspoon sugar

Dash of pepper

2 green onions, thinly sliced

holiday history

Red, symbolizing joy and celebration, is the traditional color of the Chinese New Year. During Chinese New Year, children are given bright red envelopes filled with lucky money. For fun, have some red envelopes ready with coins inside, and pass them out to the children—they'll love it.

1. Cut fish fillets into 1-inch pieces. Mix 2 teaspoons teriyaki sauce and the cornstarch. Set aside.

2. Heat wok or 12-inch skillet over high heat until hot. Add oil; rotate wok to coat side. Add tomatoes, chopped onion and garlic; stir-fry 3 minutes.

3. Stir in 1/4 cup teriyaki marinade, the wine, sugar and pepper. Heat to boiling; reduce heat. Stir in fish. Simmer uncovered 5 to 7 minutes, stirring occasionally, until fish flakes easily with fork. Stir in cornstarch mixture; cook and stir 1 minute. Stir in green onions.

one serving: Calories 145 (Calories from Fat 35); Fat 4g (Saturated 1g); Cholesterol 50mg; Sodium 600mg; Carbohydrate 8g (Dietary Fiber 1g); Protein 19g. % Daily Value: Vitamin A 8%; Vitamin C 10%; Calcium 2%; Iron 4%. Diet Exchanges: 2 Vegetable, 2 1/2 Very Lean Meat. Carbohydrate Choices: 1/2

Stir-Fried Noodles with Vegetables

PREP: 20 MINUTES • COOK: 15 MINUTES • 6 SERVINGS

1 package (8 ounces) dried Chinese noodles

2 teaspoons sesame oil

1/4 cup dry sherry or chicken broth

2 tablespoons oyster sauce

1 teaspoon sugar

1/8 teaspoon pepper

1 tablespoon vegetable oil

1 clove garlic, crushed

1 tablespoon finely chopped gingerroot

1 cup sliced fresh shiitake mushrooms

4 cups thinly sliced Chinese (napa) cabbage

2 medium carrots, shredded (1 1/2 cups)

holiday shortcut

Want to skip some chopping chores? Look for chopped, jarred gingerroot—it's a cinch to spoon into the stir-fry.

1. Cook and drain noodles as directed on package. Toss noodles and sesame oil. Mix sherry, oyster sauce, sugar and pepper.

2. Heat vegetable oil in 12-inch skillet or wok over high heat. Add garlic and gingerroot; stir-fry 30 seconds. Add mushrooms, cabbage and carrots; stir-fry 1 to 2 minutes or until crisp-tender. Stir in sherry mixture. Toss noodles and vegetable mixture, using 2 forks.

one serving: Calories 210 (Calories from Fat 45); Fat 5g (Saturated 1g); Cholesterol 0mg; Sodium 160mg; Carbohydrate 35g (Dietary Fiber 3g); Protein 6g. % Daily Value: Vitamin A 12%; Vitamin C 12%; Calcium 2%; Iron 10%. Diet Exchanges: 2 Starch, 1 Vegetable, 1/2 Fat. Carbohydrate Choices: 2

Pork Fried Rice

PREP TIME: 15 MINUTES • COOK: 10 MINUTES • 6 SERVINGS

2 tablespoons vegetable oil	1 cup cut-up cooked pork
1 cup sliced mushrooms (about 3 ounces)	2 eggs, slightly beaten
1 cup bean sprouts	3/4 cup frozen green peas, thawed
4 green onions, sliced	2 tablespoons soy sauce
3 cups cold cooked rice	Dash of pepper

1. Heat wok or 10-inch skillet over medium heat until hot. Add 1 tablespoon of the oil; rotate wok to coat side. Add mushroom; stir-fry 1 minute. Add bean sprouts, onions, rice and pork; stir-fry about 5 minutes, breaking up rice, until hot.

2. Push rice mixture to side of wok; add remaining 1 tablespoon oil to wok. Add eggs; cook and stir over medium heat until eggs are thickened throughout but still moist. Stir eggs into rice mixture.

3. Stir in peas, soy sauce and pepper. Cook until thoroughly heated.

holiday shortcut

Save time—make this rice the night before and refrigerate. Just heat up the wok and stir-fry the rice to heat through when ready to serve.

one serving: Calories 255 (Calories from Fat 90); Fat 10g (Saturated 2g); Cholesterol 90mg; Sodium 350mg; Carbohydrate 27g (Dietary Fiber 2g); Protein 14g. % Daily Value: Vitamin A 4%; Vitamin C 4%; Calcium 4%; Iron 12%. Diet Exchanges: 2 Starch, 1 Medium-Fat Meat, 1/2 Fat. Carbohydrate Choices: 2

Gingered Pineapple

PREP: 20 MINUTES • CHILL: 1 HOUR • 6 SERVINGS

1 medium pineapple, peeled and cut into chunks

1 teaspoon finely chopped gingerroot
or 1/2 teaspoon ground ginger

1 medium orange

1/4 cup flaked or shredded coconut, if desired

holiday shortcut

Don't want to tackle a whole pineapple? You can substitute 3 cups purchased fresh cubed pineapple or 3 cans (8 ounces each) pineapple chunks in juice, drained, for the fresh pineapple.

1. Place pineapple in glass or plastic dish. Sprinkle with gingerroot.

2. Finely shred 2 teaspoons orange peel; sprinkle over pineapple. Cut orange in half and remove seeds. Squeeze juice (about 1/4 cup) over pineapple. Stir gently.

3. Cover and refrigerate at least 1 hour, stirring once, to blend flavors. To serve, sprinkle with coconut.

one serving: Calories 45 (Calories from Fat 0); Fat 0g (Saturated 0g); Cholesterol 0mg; Sodium 0mg; Carbohydrate 11g (Dietary Fiber 1g); Protein 0g. % Daily Value: Vitamin A 0%; Vitamin C 26%; Calcium 0%; Iron 2%. Diet Exchanges: 1 Fruit. Carbohydrate Choices: 1

VALENTINE'S DAY

THE TRUE ORIGIN OF ST. VALENTINE'S DAY is a bit fuzzy. In addition to being associated with two early Christian martyrs named Valentine, February 14th also marked the beginning of the mating season for birds, according to the ancient Romans. The latter may help explain all the hearts, flowers and romance we now connect with the holiday. If you're looking for a heartfelt way to show your love and affection on Valentine's Day, try making the special family meal that follows. You can make the cake the night before and the stew in the morning—which gives you plenty of time to deliver all your valentine cards and kisses in person.

HEARTWARMING VALENTINE'S DAY DINNER

SERVES 6

Frozen Cranberry Margaritas

Burgundy Stew with Herb Dumplings

Tossed Green Salad

Crusty French Bread

Chocolate Sweetheart Cake

* RECIPE FOLLOWS

Frozen Cranberry Margaritas

PREP: 10 MINUTES • FREEZE: 24 HOURS • 15 SERVINGS (2/3 CUP EACH)

1 can (11 1/2 ounces) frozen cranberry juice cocktail concentrate, thawed

2 cans (12 ounces each) lemon-lime soda pop

5 cups water

1 cup tequila

1/4 cup lime juice

1. Pour all ingredients into 3-quart plastic container; beat with wire whisk or spoon until well blended.

2. Cover and freeze at least 24 hours until slushy. Serve in margarita or cocktail glasses.

one serving: Calories 90 (Calories from Fat 0); Fat 0g; (Saturated 0g); Cholesterol 0mg; Sodium 10mg; Carbohydrate 17g (Dietary Fiber 0g); Protein 0g. % Daily Value: Vitamin A 0%; Vitamin C 18%; Calcium 0%; Iron 0%. Diet Exchanges: 1 Fruit, 1/2 Fat. Carbohydrate Choices: 1

holiday FLAVOR *twist*

For the kids, mix half cranberry juice and half lemon-lime soda pop in fun glasses.

holiday DO-AHEAD *tip*

Serve this fun drink in colorful plastic beverage glasses. Attach large dots, hearts, or stripe stickers to the glasses, and let each person write their name on the stickers to identify their glasses.

Burgundy Stew with Herb Dumplings

PREP: 25 MINUTES • COOK: 10 HOURS • FINISH: 35 MINUTES • 8 SERVINGS

2 pounds beef boneless bottom or top round, cut into 1-inch pieces

4 medium carrots, cut into 1/4-inch slices (2 cups)

2 medium stalks celery, sliced (1 cup)

2 medium onions, sliced

1 can (14 1/2 ounces) diced tomatoes, undrained

1 can (6 ounces) sliced mushrooms, drained

3/4 cup dry red wine or beef broth

1 1/2 teaspoons salt

1 teaspoon dried thyme leaves

1 teaspoon ground mustard (dry)

1/4 teaspoon pepper

1/4 cup water

3 tablespoons all-purpose flour

Herb Dumplings (below)

holiday
shortcut

Carve out some extra time for Valentine's Day fun— instead of cleaning and slicing carrots, use 2 cups of baby-cut carrots.

1. Mix all ingredients except water, flour and Herb Dumplings in 3 1/2- to 6-quart slow cooker.

2. Cover and cook on low heat setting 8 to 10 hours (or high heat setting 4 to 5 hours) or until vegetables and beef are tender. Mix water and flour; gradually stir into beef mixture.

3. About 40 minutes before serving, prepare Herb Dumplings. Drop dough by spoonfuls onto hot beef mixture. Cover and cook on high heat setting 25 to 35 minutes or until toothpick inserted in center of dumplings comes out clean.

Herb Dumplings

Mix 1 1/2 cups Bisquick® Original baking mix, 1/2 teaspoon dried thyme leaves and 1/4 teaspoon dried sage leaves, crumbled. Stir in 1/2 cup milk just until baking mix is moistened.

one serving: Calories 275 (Calories from Fat 65); Fat 7g; (Saturated 2g); Cholesterol 60mg; Sodium 1030mg; Carbohydrate 26g (Dietary Fiber 3g); Protein 27g. % Daily Value: Vitamin A10%; Vitamin C 10%; Calcium 10%; Iron 20%. Diet Exchanges: 1 1/2 Starch, 1 Vegetable, 2 1/2 Lean Meat. Carbohydrate Choices: 2

Sealed-with-a-Kiss Cards

Homemade valentines are so special—why not spend an afternoon making these Valentines with the kids? The lucky recipients will treasure them!

HOW TO DO IT:

1. Apply lipstick to lips, then kiss cards and backs of envelopes.
2. Decorate as desired with paint pen.
3. Tie each card with cording into bow or "love knots."

WHAT YOU NEED:

Lipstick

Assorted plain note cards and envelopes

Red cording

Paint Pen

Chocolate Sweetheart Cake

PREP: 15 MINUTES • BAKE: 35 MINUTES • COOL: 1 HOUR 10 MINUTES • 12–16 SERVINGS

1 package (1 pound 2.25 ounces) devil's food cake mix with pudding

1 1/3 cups water

1/2 cup vegetable oil

3 eggs

1 tub (12 ounces) chocolate whipped frosting or 1 tub (16 ounces) chocolate ready-to-spread frosting

holiday
FLAVOR *twist*

For a truly special presentation to make hearts flutter, garnish with fresh small strawberries or raspberries and curls of white chocolate. Or for real chocolate lovers, press miniature chocolate chips onto the side of the frosted cake.

1. Heat oven to 350°. Grease bottom only of 1 round pan, 8 × 1 1/2 inches, and 1 square pan, 8 × 8 × 2 inches, with shortening. Make cake mix as directed on package, using water, oil and eggs. Pour into pans.

2. Bake 30 to 35 minutes or until toothpick inserted in center comes out clean. Cool 10 minutes. Run knife around sides of pans to loosen cakes; remove from pans to wire rack. Cool completely, about 1 hour.

Cut round layer in half as shown in diagram. Freeze uncovered about 1 hour for easier frosting if desired. Arrange pieces on serving platter to form heart as shown in diagram. Frost cake with frosting, attaching pieces with small amount of frosting. Store loosely covered at room temperature.

one serving: Calories 410 (Calories from Fat 190); Fat 21g; (Saturated 8g); Cholesterol 55mg; Sodium 400mg; Carbohydrate 51g (Dietary Fiber 2g); Protein 4g. % Daily Value: Vitamin A 2%; Vitamin C 0%; Calcium 6%; Iron 8%. Diet Exchanges: 1 1/2 Starch, 2 Other Carbohydrates, 4 Fat. Carbohydrate Choices: 3 1/2

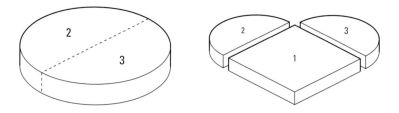

Moss Heart

Wear your heart on your wall—not on your sleeve! This pretty heart will still brighten your home even after Valentine's Day has passed. Or, make the heart for a favorite friend or relative—they will love receiving it as a valentine.

WHAT YOU NEED:

Cardboard

Hot-glue gun and glue sticks

Green floral moss

Ribbon

Dried flowers

HOW TO DO IT:

1. Cut cardboard into 7-inch heart shape.

2. Glue moss onto heart, covering completely.

3. Poke hole in top of each rounded part of heart. To hang heart, thread ribbon through each hole and tie knot. Add bows.

4. Glue flowers onto moss. Let dry.

ST. PATRICK'S DAY

ST. PATRICK, THE PATRON SAINT OF IRELAND, is credited with bringing Christianity to Ireland while still respecting the country's ancient customs and traditions. He is also said to have driven all the snakes out of the Emerald Isle. Today, most St. Patrick's Day celebrations involve far less serious and scary endeavors—such as wearing green, drinking beer and waving Irish flags. You certainly don't need the luck of the Irish to serve up this cozy dinner on March 17. It's so easy to make with your slow cooker and bread machine, you'd think a leprechaun lent you a hand in the kitchen.

HAPPY ST. PATRICK'S DAY DINNER

SERVES 8

Beet Salad with Toasted Walnuts

Corned Beef and Cabbage Dinner

Apple Rye Bread
or
Irish Soda Bread

Creamy Irish Pie

Chilled Ale

Chilled Root Beer

*RECIPE FOLLOWS

Beet Salad with Toasted Walnuts

PREP: 20 MINUTES • CHILL: 8 HOURS • 8 SERVINGS

1 tablespoon vegetable or olive oil	1/4 teaspoon salt
1/2 cup walnut pieces	1/8 teaspoon coarsely ground black pepper
3 tablespoons vegetable or olive oil	1 can (8.25 ounces) julienne beets, drained
3 tablespoons balsamic vinegar	2 green onions, sliced
1 tablespoon orange marmalade	6 cups torn leaf lettuce or mixed salad greens

1. Cook 1 tablespoon oil and the walnuts in 8-inch skillet over medium heat until walnuts are toasted, about 5 minutes, stirring occasionally. With slotted spoon, remove walnuts from skillet; place in small bowl to cool. Cover and store at room temperature.

2. Add remaining 3 tablespoons oil, the vinegar, marmalade, salt and pepper to oil in skillet; mix well. Place beets and onions in resealable plastic storage bag or container. Add vinegar mixture; toss gently to coat. Cover; refrigerate at least 8 hours but no longer than 24 hours.

3. About 15 minutes before serving, arrange lettuce on individual serving plates. Top each with marinated beet mixture. Drizzle with marinade. Sprinkle with toasted walnuts.

one serving: Calories 125 (Calories from Fat 90); Fat 10g (Saturated 1g); Cholesterol 0mg; Sodium 140mg; Carbohydrate 7g (Dietary Fiber 2g); Protein 2g. % Daily Value: Vitamin A 26%; Vitamin C 16%; Calcium 4%; Iron 8%. Diet Exchanges: 1 1/2 Vegetable, 2 Fat. Carbohydrate Choices: 1/2

holiday FLAVOR *twist*

Balsamic vinegar, made from white grape juice and aged in barrels, adds a bit of sweetness to this salad. If you don't have balsamic vinegar, use the same amount of of cider vinegar but add a pinch of brown sugar.

Corned Beef and Cabbage Dinner

PREP: 15 MINUTES • COOK: 12 HOURS • FINISH: 40 MINUTES • 8 SERVINGS

2 pounds small red potatoes

1 1/2 cups fresh baby carrots

1 medium onion, cut into 8 wedges

2 to 2 1/2-pounds corned beef brisket
with seasoning packet

2 cups apple juice

Water

8 thin green cabbage wedges

Horseradish Sauce (below)

holiday tip
DO-AHEAD

It's the luck of the Irish this
dish works so well in a
slow cooker! Just put it on
in the morning, and enjoy
a wonderful dinner at the
end of the day.

1. Place potatoes, carrots and onion in 5- to 6 1/2–quart slow cooker. Top with corned beef brisket; sprinkle with contents of seasoning packet. Add apple juice and enough water just to cover brisket.

2. Cover; cook on low setting for 10 to 12 hours.

3. About 40 minutes before serving, remove beef from slow cooker; place on serving platter and cover to keep warm. Add cabbage wedges to vegetables and broth in slow cooker. Increase heat setting to high; cover and cook an additional 30 to 35 minutes or until cabbage is crisp-tender.

4. Prepare Horseradish Sauce.

5. To serve, cut corned beef across grain into thin slices. With slotted spoon, remove vegetables from slow cooker. Serve corned beef and vegetables with sauce.

Horseradish Sauce

1/2 cup sour cream

1/4 cup mayonnaise or salad
dressing

2 tablespoons prepared horseradish

2 teaspoons Dijon mustard

Mix all ingredients together in small bowl.

one serving: Calories 415 (Calories from Fat 215); Fat 24g (Saturated 8g); Cholesterol 90mg; Sodium 630mg; Carbohydrate 37g (Dietary Fiber 6g); Protein 19g. % Daily Value: Vitamin A 90%; Vitamin C 38%; Calcium 10%; Iron 24%. Diet Exchanges: 1 Starch, 1 Fruit, 1 Vegetable, 2 High-Fat Meat, 1 Fat. Carbohydrate Choices: 2 1/2

Apple Rye Bread

PREP: 5 MINUTES • BAKE: ABOUT 3 1/2 HOURS • 1 LOAF (12 SLICES)

3/4 cup water

1/2 cup applesauce

3 tablespoons brown sugar

2 tablespoons oil

1 1/4 teaspoons salt

2 cups bread flour

1 cup rye flour

1 1/2 teaspoons bread machine or active dry yeast

holiday FLAVOR *twist*

Either sweetened or unsweetened applesauce works in this tasty bread. However, you may prefer a slightly less sweet bread to serve with spicy corned beef and cabbage so try unsweetened applesauce.

holiday DO-AHEAD *tip*

To get your timing just right, set the bread machine to delay start so the bread is done 30 minutes before dinner. That way, you'll have enough cooling time before you begin slicing the bread. A serrated bread or electric knife is best for slicing fresh bread.

1. Use bread machine that produces a 1 1/2-pound loaf. Measure ingredients carefully. Follow manufacturer's directions for placing ingredients in machine.

2. Select Basic/White cycle. Follow manufacturer's directions for staring machines.

one slice: Calories 160 (Calories from Fat 25); Fat 3g; (Saturated 0g); Cholesterol 0mg; Sodium 250mg; Carbohydrate 30g (Dietary Fiber 2g); Protein 3g. % Daily Value: Vitamin A 0%; Vitamin C 0%; Calcium 0%; Iron 8%. Diet Exchanges: 1 Starch, 1 Other Carbohydrates, 1/2 Fat. Carbohydrate Choices: 2

Irish Soda Bread

PREP: 10 MINUTES • BAKE: 45 MINUTES • COOL: 30 MINUTES • 1 LOAF (8 WEDGES)

2 1/2 cups all-purpose flour

2 tablespoons sugar

1 teaspoon baking soda

1 teaspoon baking powder

1/2 teaspoon salt

3 tablespoons butter or margarine, softened

1/3 cup raisins

About 1 cup buttermilk

Additional softened butter, if desired

1. Heat oven to 375°. Grease cookie sheet with shortening. Mix flour, sugar, baking soda, baking powder and salt in large bowl. Cut in 3 tablespoons butter, using pastry blender or crisscrossing 2 knives, until mixture looks like fine crumbs. Stir in raisins and just enough buttermilk so dough leaves side of bowl.

2. Place dough on lightly floured surface; gently roll in flour to coat. Knead 1 to 2 minutes or until smooth. Shape into round loaf, about 6 1/2 inches in diameter. Place on cookie sheet. Cut an X shape about 1/2 inch deep through loaf with floured knife.

3. Bake 35 to 45 minutes or until golden brown. Remove from cookie sheet to wire rack. Brush with additional softened butter. Cool completely, about 30 minutes, before cutting.

one wedge: Calories 220 (Calories from Fat 45); Fat 5g (Saturated 3g); Cholesterol 15mg; Sodium 420mg; Carbohydrate 39g (Dietary Fiber 1g); Protein 5g. % Daily Value: Vitamin A 4%; Vitamin C 0%; Calcium 8%; Iron 10%. Diet Exchanges: 1 1/2 Starch, 1 Fruit, 1 Fat. Carbohydrate Choices: 2 1/2

holiday history

This classic Irish soda bread is easy to make and best served fresh. Don't forget to cut the traditional X on top before baking. It represents a cross, which, according to legend, helps scare the devil away.

Creamy Irish Pie

PREP: 45 MINUTES • CHILL: 4 HOURS • 8 SERVINGS

Chocolate Pat-in-Pan Pie Crust (below)

1/2 cup milk

32 large jet-puffed marshmallows

1/3 cup Irish cream liqueur

1 1/2 cups whipping (heavy) cream

Grated semisweet baking chocolate, if desired

holiday
FLAVOR *twist*

No Irish cream liqueur? Just substitute 3 tablespoons Irish-style flavored instant coffee mix (dry). Stir it into the melted marshmallow mixture until dissolved.

1. Heat oven to 400°. Bake and cool Chocolate Pat-in-Pan Pie Crust.

2. Heat milk and marshmallows in 3-quart saucepan over low heat, stirring constantly, just until marshmallows are melted. Refrigerate about 20 minutes, stirring occasionally, until mixture mounds slightly on spoon. (If mixture becomes too thick, place saucepan in bowl of warm water; stir mixture until proper consistency.) Gradually stir in liqueur.

3. Beat whipping cream in chilled medium bowl with electric mixer on high speed until soft peaks form. Fold marshmallow mixture into whipped cream. Spread in pie crust. Sprinkle with chocolate. Cover and refrigerate at least 4 hours until set but no longer than 48 hours. Store covered in refrigerator.

Chocolate Pat-in-Pan Pie Crust

3/4 cup plus 2 tablespoons all-purpose flour

1/2 cup butter or margarine, softened

1/4 cup powdered sugar

1/4 cup finely chopped pecans or walnuts

2 tablespoons baking cocoa

Mix all ingredients in medium bowl until soft dough forms. Press firmly and evenly against bottom and side of ungreased pie plate, 9 × 1 1/4 inches. Bake 12 to 15 minutes or until golden brown. Cool completely.

one serving: Calories 445 (Calories from Fat 250); Fat 28g (Saturated 16g); Cholesterol 80mg; Sodium 115mg; Carbohydrate 44g (Dietary Fiber 1g); Protein 4g. % Daily Value: Vitamin A 19%; Vitamin C 0%; Calcium 6%; Iron 6%. Diet Exchanges: 1 Starch, 2 Other Carbohydrates, 5 1/2 Fat. Carbohydrate Choices: 3

Cabbage Leaf Bouquet

This fresh look at a St. Patrick's Day centerpiece makes masterful use of cabbage—it's a fun companion to the corned beef and cabbage you'll be serving.

WHAT YOU NEED:

1 floral water tube

1 single flower stem (such as freesia, Alstroemeria or rose), 4 to 5 inches long

1 leaf red kale or savoy cabbage, 4 × 5 inches

12 inches 1/4- to 1/2-inch-wide ribbon or several strands 12-inch-long raffia

HOW TO DO IT:

1. Fill water tube with water; add cap and insert flower stem.

2. Wrap leaf around tube. Wrap ribbon around stem end, and tie a bow.

EASTER

FOR CHRISTIANS AROUND THE WORLD, Easter commemorates the resurrection of Christ. It is widely celebrated as a day of joy and rebirth. These themes of rebirth and renewal are echoed by the changing season, with its freshly emerging flowers, budding trees and retreating frost. And where, you may ask, do the Easter Bunny and eggs fit into the picture? They are symbols of fertility and new life. So tie on your favorite Easter bonnet, send the kids scavenging for brightly colored eggs and other goodies and enjoy this hoppy, er happy, holiday with your family and friends.

HAPPY EASTER DINNER

SERVES 6

*Strawberry Spinach Salad

*Minted Leg of Lamb

*Green Beans with Browned Butter

*Best Mashed Potatoes

*Rainbow Egg Cookies

*Easter Bunny Cake

White Wine

*RECIPE FOLLOWS

Strawberry Spinach Salad

PREP: 15 MINUTES • 6 SERVINGS

Orange Honey Dressing (below)

6 cups bite-size pieces spinach

1 cup sliced strawberries

1/3 cup sliced green onions

1 can (11 ounces) mandarin orange segments, drained

2 tablespoons pine nuts

1. Prepare Orange Honey Dressing.

2. Toss dressing and remaining ingredients except pine nuts. Sprinkle with pine nuts.

Orange Honey Dressing

2 tablespoons orange juice

2 tablespoons honey

1 tablespoon vegetable oil

1 teaspoon Dijon mustard

Shake all ingredients in tightly covered container.

one serving: Calories 115 (Calories from Fat 35); Fat 4g; (Saturated 1g); Cholesterol 0mg; Sodium 45mg; Carbohydrate 18g (Dietary Fiber 2g); Protein 2g. % Daily Value: Vitamin A 26%; Vitamin C 64%; Calcium 4%; Iron 8%. Diet Exchanges: 1 Vegetable, 1 Fruit, 1 Fat. Carbohydrate Choices: 1

holiday
FLAVOR *twist*

Toasting pine nuts intensifies their flavor. To toast, cook in ungreased heavy skillet over medium-low heat 5 to 7 minutes, stirring frequently until browning begins, then stirring constantly until golden brown.

Minted Leg of Lamb

PREP: 20 MINUTES • MARINATE: 8 HOURS • ROAST: 2 1/2 HOURS • 8 SERVINGS

1/2 cup packed brown sugar

1/4 cup chopped fresh mint leaves

1/2 cup vegetable oil

1 teaspoon grated lemon peel

1/4 cup lemon juice

1 tablespoon chopped fresh or 1 teaspoon dried tarragon leaves

3 tablespoons white vinegar

1 teaspoon salt

1 teaspoon ground mustard (dry)

4- to 5-pound leg of lamb

Lamb Gravy (below)

holiday shortcut

Carving can be quick and easy if you know how.

Place leg shank bone to your right, on carving board or platter. (Place shank bone to your left if you are left-handed.) Cut a few length-wise slices from thin side. Turn leg, cut side down, so it rests firmly. Make vertical slices to the leg bone, then cut horizontally along bone to release slices.

1. Mix all ingredients except leg of lamb and Lamb Gravy. Heat to boiling; reduce heat. Simmer 5 minutes; cool.

2. Place lamb in plastic bag or shallow glass dish. Pour cooled marinade over lamb. Fasten bag securely or cover dish with plastic wrap. Refrigerate at least 8 hours but no longer than 24 hours, turning lamb occasionally.

3. Heat oven to 325°. Place lamb, fat side up, on rack in shallow roasting pan. Insert meat thermometer so tip is in center of thickest part of lamb and does not touch bone or rest in fat. Roast uncovered 2 to 2 1/2 hours or until desired degree of doneness. (Thermometer should read 170° to 180°.) Remove lamb to heated platter; keep warm. Prepare Lamb Gravy; serve with lamb.

Lamb Gravy

Strain drippings from roasting pan. Remove fat, reserving 2 table-spoons. Add enough water to drippings to measure 2 cups liquid. Stir 2 tablespoons all-purpose flour into reserved fat in 1 1/2-quart saucepan. Cook over low heat, stirring constantly, until smooth and bubbly; remove from heat. Stir in liquid. Heat to boiling, stirring constantly. Boil and stir 1 minute.

one serving: Calories 415 (Calories from Fat 225); Fat 25g; (Saturated 6g); Cholesterol 105mg; Sodium 380mg; Carbohydrate 16g (Dietary Fiber 0g); Protein 32g. % Daily Value: Vitamin A 2%; Vitamin C 2%; Calcium 2%; Iron 16%. Diet Exchanges: 1 Starch, 4 Medium-Fat Meat, 1 Fat. Carbohydrate Choices: 1

Robin's Eggs in Nest Centerpiece

This charming nest adds a wonderful spring touch to your table, and it also looks terrific with Easter baskets.

WHAT YOU NEED:

- 1 dozen uncooked eggs in carton
- Rubber gloves
- Plastic to protect table
- Medium-blue craft paint
- Small paintbrush
- Brown craft paint
- Soft blue or patterned fabric (enough to cover box)
- Bottom of cardboard gift box
- Fabric stiffener (available at craft and fabric stores)
- Natural shredded packing material (excelsior)

HOW TO DO IT:

1. Punch a hole the size of a nickel in end or side of egg. Drain out contents; rinse and let dry in egg carton.

2. Wearing gloves and working over plastic, squirt a small amount of blue paint into palm, then roll egg in hands until it becomes a mottled blue. Dip handle end of paintbrush into brown paint, and dab dots onto blue eggs. Let dry.

3. Cut enough fabric to fit over box bottom and fold over sides. Soak fabric in stiffener; ring out fabric, fold over box bottom and let dry. Add packing material and eggs to box "nest."

Green Beans with Browned Butter

PREP: 10 MINUTES • COOK: 15 MINUTES • 6 SERVINGS (1/2 CUP EACH)

3/4 pound green beans, cut in half

2 tablespoons butter*

2 tablespoons pine nuts

1 teaspoon grated lemon peel

holiday FLAVOR *twist*

Sliced or slivered almonds or chopped pecans or walnuts are tasty substitutes for the pine nuts. Once the butter begins to brown, it browns very quickly and can burn, so use low heat and a watchful eye.

1. Place beans in 1 inch water in 2 1/2-quart saucepan. Heat to boiling; reduce heat. Simmer uncovered 8 to 10 minutes or until crisp-tender; drain. Keep warm.

2. Meanwhile, melt butter in 1-quart saucepan over low heat. Stir in pine nuts. Heat, stirring constantly, until butter is golden brown. Immediately remove from heat. Pour butter mixture over beans; toss to coat. Sprinkle with lemon peel.

*Do not use margarine because it doesn't brown or have the flavor of browned butter.

one serving: Calories 45 (Calories from Fat 45); Fat 5g; (Saturated 3g); Cholesterol 10mg; Sodium 30mg; Carbohydrate 4g (Dietary Fiber 2g); Protein 1g. % Daily Value: Vitamin A 8%; Vitamin C 0%; Calcium 2%; Iron 4%. Diet Exchanges: 1 Vegetable, 1 Fat. Carbohydrate Choices: 0

Best Mashed Potatoes

PREP: 10 MINUTES • COOK: 30 MINUTES • 6 SERVINGS

2 pounds potatoes, peeled if desired

1/3 to 1/2 cup milk

1/4 cup butter or margarine, softened

1/2 teaspoon salt

Dash of pepper

1. Place potatoes in 2-quart saucepan; add enough water just to cover potatoes. Heat to boiling; reduce heat. Cover and simmer 20 to 30 minutes or until potatoes are tender; drain. Shake pan with potatoes over low heat to dry (this will help mashed potatoes be fluffier).

2. Mash potatoes in pan until no lumps remain. Add milk in small amounts, mashing after each addition (amount of milk needed to make potatoes smooth and fluffy depends on kind of potatoes used).

3. Add butter, salt and pepper. Mash vigorously until potatoes are light and fluffy. If desired, sprinkle with small pieces of butter or sprinkle with paprika, chopped fresh parsley or chives.

one serving: Calories 250 (Calories from Fat 110); Fat 12g (Saturated 7g); Cholesterol 30mg; Sodium 390mg; Carbohydrate 31g (Dietary Fiber 2g); Protein 4g. % Daily Value: Vitamin A 10%; Vitamin C 14%; Calcium 4%; Iron 2%. Diet Exchanges: 2 Starch, 2 Fat. Carbohydrate Choices: 2

holiday FLAVOR *twist*

Make these yummy potatoes your way—choose any one of these easy variations for deliciously different potatoes. Why not make a double batch—these potatoes will go fast!

blue cheese mashed potatoes: Stir in 1/4 cup crumbled blue cheese in step 3.

garlic mashed potatoes: Cook 6 cloves garlic, peeled, with the potatoes.

horseradish mashed potatoes: Add 2 tablespoons prepared mild or hot horseradish with the butter, salt and pepper in step 3.

Easter Egg Cookie Hunt

Want a fun new way to enjoy an Easter egg hunt? Try these incredibly cute cookies—the kids will love making them, hiding them . . . and finding them. Tuck the cookies in small plastic or cellophane bags and tie with pastel ribbons to keep them fresh and to allow you to hide them safely in all kinds of places.

Rainbow Egg Cookies

18 Sandwich Cookies

WHAT YOU NEED:

1 pouch (1 pound 1.5 ounces) sugar cookie mix

1/2 cup butter or margarine, melted

1/4 cup all-purpose flour

1 egg

3 food colors

White coarse sugar crystals or granulated sugar, if desired

1/2 tub (16 ounce size) vanilla ready-to-spread frosting

HOW TO DO IT:

1. Heat oven to 375°. Stir cookie mix, margarine, flour and egg until soft dough forms. Divide dough evenly among 3 bowls; tint each dough by stirring in a few drops of desired food color. (See Food Colors chart on opposite page for a guide to mixing colors. For a variety of colors, make several batches of cookies.)

2. Shape 1/3 cup of each color of dough into a rope about 5 inches long and 1 inch in diameter. Place ropes side by side and a little more than 1/4 inch apart on floured surface; roll until 1/4 inch thick. Cut with 2- to 2 1/2-inch egg-shaped cookie cutter so each cookie has 3 colors. Sprinkle with sugar. Place 2 inches apart on ungreased cookie sheet. Repeat with remaining dough. (When rerolling dough scraps, carefully lay matching colors together. For marbled cookies, mix colors of dough scraps—but don't mix colors too much or they won't be distinct.)

3. Bake 7 to 9 minutes or until edges are light golden brown. Cool 1 minute; remove from cookie sheet to wire rack. Cool completely, about 30 minutes. Spread frosting on bottoms of half the cookies. Top with remaining cookies.

Food Colors

Two types of food color are widely available: liquid and paste. *Liquid* food colors are easy to find at your supermarket. *Paste* colors can be found in cake decorating or specialty food stores. You may prefer paste colors because they are much more vivid than liquid colors. Paste food colors are used in this recipe.

When using liquid food color, go slowly to get the exact shade of color you want. Add one drop at a time, and mix it into the dough or frosting completely before adding more color.

To make the colors of Rainbow Egg Cookies with liquid food colors, use the proportions of liquid food color in the chart below as a guide.

COLOR	NUMBER OF DROPS OF LIQUID FOOD COLOR
Orange	2 drops yellow and 2 drops red
Peach	4 drops yellow and 1 drop red
Lime Green	3 drops yellow and 1 drop green
Turquoise Blue	3 drops blue and 1 drop green
Purple	3 drops red and 2 drops blue
Rose	5 drops red and 1 drop blue

Easter Bunny Cake

PREP: 30 MINUTES • BAKE: 30 MINUTES • COOL: 1 HOUR 10 MINUTES • 8 SERVINGS

1 package (1 pound 2 ounces) carrot cake mix with pudding

1 cup water

1/2 cup vegetable oil

3 eggs

1 tub (12 ounces) cream cheese whipped frosting or 1 tub (16 ounces) vanilla ready-to-spread frosting

1 cup flaked or shredded coconut

Pink construction paper

Jelly beans or small gumdrops

holiday FLAVOR *twist*

Make a pretty lawn for your bunny cake with this easy green "grass." To make the grass, shake 1 cup coconut and 3 drops green food color in tightly covered jar until evenly tinted.

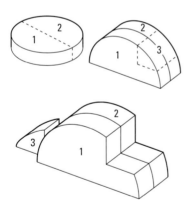

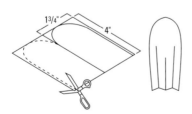

1. Heat oven to 350°. Grease bottoms only of 2 round pans, 8 or 9 × 1 1/2 inches, with shortening. Make cake mix as directed on package, using water, oil and eggs. Pour into pans.

2. Bake 8-inch rounds 25 to 30 minutes, 9-inch rounds 22 to 27 minutes, or until toothpick inserted in center comes out clean. Cool 10 minutes. Run knife around side of pans to loosen cakes; remove from pans to wire rack. Cool completely, about 1 hour.

3. Reserve 1 cake layer for another use or to make a second bunny. Cut 1 cake layer in half as shown in diagram. Freeze pieces uncovered about 1 hour for easier frosting if desired. Cover large flat tray or piece of cardboard with aluminum foil. Put halves together with frosting to form body. Place rounded side up on tray.

4. Cut out a piece about one-third of the way up one edge of body to form tail as shown in diagram. Attach tail with toothpick. Frost bunny with remaining frosting, rounding out head and body. Sprinkle with coconut. Cut ears from construction paper; press into head. Use jelly beans for eyes and nose. Store loosely covered at room temperature.

one serving: Calories 350 (Calories from Fat 160); Fat 18g; (Saturated 6g); Cholesterol 45mg; Sodium 300mg; Carbohydrate 45g (Dietary Fiber 1g); Protein 3g. % Daily Value: Vitamin A 4%; Vitamin C 0%; Calcium 4%; Iron 4%. Diet Exchanges: 1 Starch, 2 Other Carbohydrates, 4 1/2 Fat. Carbohydrate Chocies: 3

Flower Table Card

Spring has definitely sprung when you place these fresh cards on the table. They also make wonderful gifts for guests to take home.

WHAT YOU NEED:

1 piece art cardboard or mat board, 13 × 18 inches or desired size

1 piece heavy paper (such as wrapping paper or wallpaper), 12 × 17 inches or desired size

Hot-glue gun or spray adhesive

Paper punch

1 large flower blossom (such as lily, Alstroemeria, iris or small hydrangea)

1 floral water tube

24 inches 1-inch-wide ribbon, cut in half

HOW TO DO IT:

1. Fold cardboard and paper lengthwise in half. Glue paper onto cardboard.

2. Punch 1 hole on one side of card. Place flower stem in hole and then in the filled, capped water tube (under fold of card).

3. Punch holes in each end of card. Thread ribbon through holes, and tie a bow.

PASSOVER

PASSOVER IS AN EIGHT-DAY FESTIVAL that remembers the Exodus, or the release of the Israelites from centuries of slavery in Egypt during the reign of Pharaoh Ramses II. The Israelites, led by Moses, had to leave Egypt in such a hurry that there was no time to let dough rise for bread. In remembrance of this fact, modern-day Jews refrain from eating foods made with leavening and eat special bread called matza during the celebration. A ceremonial dinner, called a *Seder*, honors the traditions of Passover with special foods, songs and prayers. This special dinner menu uses no flour—just matzo meal, and ground almonds for the brownies.

CELEBRATE PASSOVER

SERVES 4

*Sautéed Chicken Paprika

*Easy Carrot Tzimmes

*Potato Kugel Puffs

*Mocha Brownie Torte with Strawberries

*RECIPE FOLLOWS

Olive Tree Centerpiece

Olives, a symbol of peace, have always had a respected place in Jewish life and culture. Try making these easy, marinated green olives, then turning them into an attractive centerpiece for a Seder table. The kids will love placing the olives almost as much as they love eating them!

HOW TO DO IT:

1. Mix olives, oil, orange peel, juice and marmalade. Cover and refrigerate 3 to 4 hours.

2. Press topiary base securely in flowerpot (glue if necessary). Fill pot 2/3 full with rocks. Insert toothpicks into topiary cone; place olives on toothpicks.

3. Line top of pot with tissue paper; cover with peanuts.

WHAT YOU NEED:

5 jars (7 ounces each) pitted queen-size green olives, drained

3 cups olive or vegetable oil

1/2 cup grated orange peel

1/2 cup orange juice

1 cup orange marmalade, melted

8-inch cone-shaped florists' foam topiary with dowel and base

Flowerpot to fit topiary base (about 5 inches in diameter)

Rocks (to weight flowerpot)

Toothpicks

Tissue paper

2 cups honey-roasted peanuts

Sautéed Chicken Paprika

PREP: 10 MINUTES • COOK: 25 MINUTES • 4 SERVINGS

3 tablespoons matzo meal

1 tablespoon paprika

1 teaspoon dry mustard

1/4 teaspoon salt

1/4 teaspoon pepper

4 boneless, skinless chicken breast halves

3 teaspoons peanut oil

1 teaspoon peanut oil

1/3 cup chopped onion

2 cloves garlic, finely chopped

3/4 cup chicken broth

1/4 cup white wine

1 small tomato, chopped

Chopped fresh parsley, if desired

holiday
FLAVOR *twist*

Serving more than four?
This recipe doubles easily,
so you can easily feed
extra friends and family.

1. Mix matzo meal, paprika, dry mustard, salt and pepper in medium bowl. Evenly coat chicken with matzo meal mixture, reserving any remaining mixture.

2. Heat 3 teaspoons oil in 10-inch nonstick skillet over medium heat until hot. Add chicken; cook 1 to 2 minutes on each side or until lightly browned. Remove chicken from skillet; keep warm.

3. In same skillet, heat remaining 1 teaspoon oil. Add onion and garlic; cook and stir until onion is tender, about 5 minutes. Add broth, wine and reserved matzo mixture; mix well. Return chicken to skillet. Bring to a boil. Reduce heat; cover and simmer 7 to 9 minutes or until chicken is fork tender and juices run clear.

4. Stir in tomato; cover and cook 2 to 3 minutes or until heated. Garnish with parsley.

one serving: Calories 235 (Calories from Fat 80); Fat 9g (Saturated 2g); Cholesterol 75mg; Sodium 410mg; Carbohydrate 9g (Dietary Fiber 1g); Protein 29g. % Daily Value: Vitamin A 26%; Vitamin C 6%; Calcium 2%; Iron 10%. Diet Exchanges: 1/2 Starch, 4 Very Lean Meat, 1 Fat. Carbohydrate Choices: 1/2

Easy Carrot Tzimmes

PREP: 10 MINUTES • COOK: 20 MINUTES • 6 SERVINGS (1/2 CUP EACH)

3 cups carrots, thinly sliced (about 1 pound)

1/2 cup water

1 cooking apple, peeled, cored and coarsely chopped

1/4 cup honey

1 tablespoon frozen orange juice concentrate, thawed

2 teaspoons margarine

1/4 teaspoon salt

1/8 teaspoon pepper

holiday FLAVOR *twist*

Tzimmes are versatile as well as delicious. You can use sweet potatoes in place of the carrots. Family members often add their own special touch to Tzimmes. A mom might toss in 1/4 cup seedless raisins. A grandma might follow an old family recipe and use sweet potatoes in place of the carrots. Or a kid could add his or her favorite snack fruit, like 1/2 cup dried apricots.

1. Heat carrots and water to boiling in 2 1/2-quart saucepan. Reduce heat; cover and simmer about 5 minutes or until crisp–tender. Drain. Remove carrots from saucepan; keep warm.

2. In same saucepan, combine remaining ingredients. Cook over low heat, stirring occasionally, about 5 minutes or until apple is tender. Add carrots; stir gently to coat. Cook until thoroughly heated.

one serving: Calories 100 (Calories from Fat 10); Fat 1g (Saturated 1g); Cholesterol 5mg; Sodium 130mg; Carbohydrate 22g (Dietary Fiber 2g); Protein 1g. % Daily Value: Vitamin A 100%; Vitamin C 8%; Calcium 2%; Iron 2%. Diet Exchanges: 1 Fruit, 2 Vegetable. Carbohydrate Choices: 1 1/2

Potato Kugel Puffs

PREP: 20 MINUTES • BAKE: 25 MINUTES • COOL: 2 MINUTES • 12 SERVINGS

2 tablespoons margarine

1 medium onion, chopped (about 1/2 cup)

1 medium carrot, finely shredded

2 1/2 cups water

1 package (6 ounces) potato pancake mix*

2 tablespoons matzo meal

1 teaspoon dried parsley flakes

1/8 teaspoon ground nutmeg

1/8 teaspoon pepper

2 egg whites

1. Heat oven to 425°. Grease 1 large or 2 medium cookie sheets.

2. Heat margarine, onion, carrot and water to boiling in 1 1/2-quart saucepan. Reduce heat; cover and simmer 2 minutes.

3. Mix pancake mix, matzo meal, parsley, nutmeg and pepper in medium bowl. Add hot vegetable mixture; stir until blended. Beat egg whites in medium bowl until stiff peaks form. Fold egg whites into potato mixture until well blended.

4. Spoon mixture onto cookie sheet, forming 12 mounds. Flatten each mound slightly to a 3-inch circle, about 1/2 inch thick.

5. Bake at 425° for 20 to 25 minutes or until light golden brown. Cool 1 to 2 minutes; remove from cookie sheet. Serve immediately, bottom side up.

*Potato pancake mix that is kosher for Passover is available where other Passover products are sold.

one serving: Calories 65 (Calories from Fat 35); Fat 4g (Saturated 2g); Cholesterol 25mg; Sodium 80mg; Carbohydrate 5g (Dietary Fiber 0g); Protein 2g. % Daily Value: Vitamin A 4%; Vitamin C 0%; Calcium 0%; Iron 0%. Diet Exchanges: 1/2 Other Carbohydrates, 1 Fat. Carbohydrate Choices: 1/2

holiday
FLAVOR *twist*

Add even more delicious flavor to these airy potato treats by topping them with Ginger Applesauce (page 188.)

Mocha Brownie Torte with Strawberries

PREP: 10 MINUTES • BAKE: 25 MINUTES • COOL: 2 HOURS 10 MINUTES • 8 SERVINGS

3/4 cup sugar

1/3 cup baking cocoa

1/3 cup margarine, softened

1/3 cup matza cake meal*

1/3 cup ground almonds

2 teaspoons instant coffee granules or crystals

1 tablespoon water

2 egg whites

1 1/2 cups sliced strawberries

2 tablespoons currant or apple jelly, melted

holiday history

The Passover matza—a cracker-like flatbread made without yeast or any other leavening—is meant to recall the Jews' escape from Egypt. Too hurried to wait for dough to rise, families baked their bread flat and ate it on the run. During Passover, to remember this long-ago event, matza is eaten instead of bread. In addition, flour, baking powder and other ingredients that go into regular breads are replaced with matza meal. The special effort of giving up bread and flour, all help keep the memory of the Exodus alive.

1. Heat oven to 350°. Line 9-inch round cake pan with waxed paper or parchment paper; grease paper.

2. Beat sugar, cocoa and butter in medium bowl until well blended. Stir cake meal, almonds, instant coffee and water into sugar mixture until smooth. (Batter will be thick.)

3. Beat egg whites in medium bowl until stiff peaks form. Fold into chocolate mixture until well blended. Spread mixture evenly in greased pan.

4. Bake at 350° for 20 to 25 minutes or until toothpick inserted in center comes out clean. Cool 10 minutes. Remove from pan; cool completely on wire rack.

5. Just before serving; place torte on serving plate. Top with sliced strawberries; brush with melted jelly. Store any remaining torte in refrigerator.

*If matza cake meal is unavailable, process matza meal in food processor bowl with metal blade until very fine.

one serving: Calories 230 (Calories from Fat 90); Fat 9g (Saturated 5g); Cholesterol 20mg; Sodium 70mg; Carbohydrate 32g (Dietary Fiber 3g); Protein 3g. % Daily Value: Vitamin A 6%; Vitamin C 30%; Calcium 2%; Iron 6%. Diet Exchanges: 1 Starch, 1 Fruit, 2 Fat. Carbohydrate Choices: 2

CINCO DE MAYO

MAY 5TH MARKS AN IMPORTANT DATE in Mexico's history. It was on that day in 1862 when the *Batalla de Puebla* took place in the little town of Puebla. In a David versus Goliath scenario, a group of Mexican soldiers made up in spirit what they lacked in equipment when they defeated an invasion of French forces, famed for being the greatest in the world. The French army, led by Napoleon III, was trying to capture Mexico City and bring the country under French rule. And, while France did eventually succeed in conquering Mexico, the surprising defeat on May 5th has become a symbol of Mexican patriotism and pride. Join in the fiesta by preparing this easy Mexican-themed menu. Olé!

CINCO DE MAYO FIESTA

SERVES 6

*White Sangria

Mexican Beer

Chilled Cola Sodas

*Chili Cheese Empanaditas

*Quick Guacamole

*Tijuana Caesar Salad

*Grilled Mexican Citrus Chicken

*Adobe Pie

Warm Flour Tortillas

*Tres Leches Cake

*RECIPE FOLLOWS

White Sangria

1/2 cup sugar

1 cup orange-flavored liqueur or orange juice

1 cup vodka or lemon-lime soda pop

2 medium peaches or nectarines, thinly sliced

1 medium orange, thinly sliced

1 lemon, thinly sliced

1 lime, thinly sliced

1 bottle (750 milliliters) dry white wine, nonalcoholic white wine or white grape juice, chilled (3 cups)

1 bottle (1 quart 1.8 ounces) club soda chilled (4 cups)

1. Stir sugar, orange liqueur and vodka in half-gallon glass or plastic pitcher until sugar is dissolved. Pour half of vodka mixture into another half-gallon glass or plastic pitcher. Divide fruits and wine evenly between pitchers.

2. Refrigerate until serving. Just before serving, pour half of club soda into each pitcher; stir gently to mix. Serve immediately. Serve over ice if desired.

one serving: Calories 140 (Calories from Fat 0); Fat 0g; (Saturated 0g); Cholesterol 0mg; Sodium 5mg; Carbohydrate 13g (Dietary Fiber 0g); Protein 0g. % Daily Value: Vitamin A 0%; Vitamin C 20%; Calcium 0%; Iron 2%. Diet Exchanges: 1 Fruit, 1 1/2 Fat. Carbohydrate Choices: 1

holiday DO-AHEAD *tip*

If you're bringing this drink to a party, pour the vodka mixture into two large Thermoses containers. Carry the club soda separately and mix just before serving.

holiday FLAVOR *twist*

The nice thing about this fruity, refreshing drink is that inexpensive liqueur, vodka and wine can be used because the flavor doesn't rely solely upon alcohol. Try Triple Sec for the orange liqueur and Chablis Blanc or Chardonnay for the dry white wine.

CINCO DE MAYO

Chili Cheese Empanaditas

PREP: 30 MINUTES • BAKE: 14 MINUTES • 32 APPETIZERS

1 package (15 ounces) refrigerated pie crusts

3/4 cup finely shredded Mexican-style four-cheese blend (3 ounces)

1/3 cup canned diced green chiles, drained

Yellow cornmeal

1 egg

1 tablespoon water

Chili powder

Sour cream, if desired

Taco sauce, if desired

holiday *shortcut*

Although the egg wash adds a beautiful glaze to the empanaditas, if time is short, you can omit that step and just sprinkle them with chili powder before baking.

holiday *tip*
DO-AHEAD

Unbaked empanaditas can be frozen for up to two months. Place them on cookie sheets and freeze until firm. Transfer to a resealable plastic food-storage bag. Bake frozen empanaditas at 400° for 12 to 17 minutes.

1. Let pie crusts stand at room temperature 5 to 10 minutes. Heat oven to 400°. Mix cheese and chiles.

2. Unfold one pie crust, placing on surface lightly dusted with cornmeal. Roll to a 13-inch circle. Cut into sixteen 3-inch rounds, rerolling scraps as necessary. Repeat with remaining pie crust.

3. Spoon 1 teaspoon cheese mixture onto center of each pastry round. Moisten edges of pastry with water; fold pastry in half over filling. Seal edge with fork. Place on ungreased cookie sheet.

4. Lightly beat egg and water. Brush mixture on pastries; sprinkle with chili powder.

5. Bake 12 to 14 minutes or until golden brown. Serve warm with sour cream and taco sauce.

one appetizer: Calories 80 (Calories from Fat 45); Fat 5g; (Saturated 2g); Cholesterol 10mg; Sodium 140mg; Carbohydrate 7g (Dietary Fiber 0g); Protein 2g. % Daily Value: Vitamin A 0%; Vitamin C 0%; Calcium 2%; Iron 2%. Diet Exchanges: 1/2 Starch, 1 Fat. Carbohydrate Choices: 1/2

Quick Guacamole

PREP: 10 MINUTES • 16 SERVINGS (2 TABLESPOONS EACH)

2 large avocados, mashed

1 tablespoon lime juice

1/3 cup thick 'n chunky salsa

Tortilla chips, if desired

holiday
FLAVOR *twist*

The lime juice not only adds flavor but helps keep the color of the mashed avocados from darkening. If you don't have any lime juice, you can use lemon juice. Add it to the mashed avocado as soon as possible.

1. Mix avocados, lime juice and salsa in glass or plastic bowl.

2. Serve with tortilla chips. Cover and refrigerate any remaining dip.

one serving: Calories 45 (Calories from Fat 35); Fat 4g; (Saturated 1g); Cholesterol 0mg; Sodium 25mg; Carbohydrate 2g (Dietary Fiber 1g); Protein 1g. % Daily Value: Vitamin A 0%; Vitamin C 4%; Calcium 0%; Iron 2%. Diet Exchanges: 1 Fat. Carbohydrate Choices: 0

Tortilla Servers

Create a festive party with tortilla shells. They make fun and colorful containers for toppings.

HOW TO DO IT:

1. Wrap each tortilla into a cone. Secure the cones with toothpicks and place in a sturdy glass.

2. Fill the tortillas with your favorite toppings, like guacamole or salsa.

WHAT YOU NEED:

Tortilla shells (use different colors like roasted red pepper, spinach or blue corn)

Toothpicks

Sturdy Glasses or containers

Tijuana Caesar Salad

PREP: 20 MINUTES • BAKE: 9 MINUTES • 4 SERVINGS

Cooking spray

3 flour tortillas (6 to 8 inches in diameter)

1/2 teaspoon garlic salt

1/2 teaspoon ground cumin

1/3 cup Caesar dressing

2 tablespoons grated lemon peel

1 tablespoon lemon juice

6 cups bite-size pieces romaine (6 ounces)

4 ounces jicama, cut into cubes (1 cup)

1 medium red bell pepper, cut into thin strips (1 cup)

1/4 cup shredded Parmesan cheese

holiday
FLAVOR *twist*

Shrimp are plentiful in Mexico, so for an authentic variation, try adding 1/2 pound cooked small shrimp to this salad.

1. Heat oven to 375°. Spray cookie sheet with cooking spray. Spray tortillas lightly with cooking spray. Sprinkle with garlic salt and cumin. Cut each tortilla in half, then crosswise into 1/2-inch strips. Place on cookie sheet. Bake 7 to 9 minutes or until crisp.

2. Mix dressing, lemon peel and lemon juice. Toss romaine, jicama, bell pepper, tortilla strips, cheese and dressing mixture in large bowl. Sprinkle with additional shredded Parmesan cheese if desired. Serve immediately.

one serving: Calories 190 (Calories from Fat 100); Fat 11g; (Saturated 3g); Cholesterol 10mg; Sodium 520mg; Carbohydrate 17g (Dietary Fiber 4g); Protein 6g. % Daily Value: Vitamin A 54%; Vitamin C 100%; Calcium 14%; Iron 8%. Diet Exchanges: 1/2 Starch, 2 Vegetables, 2 Fat. Carbohydrate Choices: 1

Grilled Mexican Citrus Chicken

PREP: 15 MINUTES • MARINATE: 3 HOURS • GRILL: 1 HOUR • 6 SERVINGS

Mexican Citrus Marinade (below)   3- to 3 1/2-pound cut-up broiler-fryer chicken

holiday shortcut

Want to get the fiesta started sooner? Use six boneless, skinless chicken breast halves instead of the cut-up broiler-fryer chicken. You can marinate them as briefly as 30 minutes but no longer than 3 hours. Then throw them on the grill—they will only take 15 to 20 minutes to cook. Olé!

1. Prepare Mexican Citrus Marinade in shallow glass or plastic dish or resealable plastic bag. Add chicken; turn to coat with marinade. Cover dish or seal bag and refrigerate, turning chicken occasionally, at least 3 hours but no longer than 24 hours.

2. Heat coals or gas grill. Remove chicken from marinade; reserve marinade. Cover and grill chicken, skin sides up, 4 to 5 inches from medium heat 15 to 20 minutes.

3. Turn. Cover and grill 20 to 40 minutes longer, turning and brushing 2 to 3 times with marinade, until juice of chicken is no longer pink when centers of the darkest pieces are cut. Discard any remaining marinade.

Mexican Citrus Marinade

1/4 cup orange juice

1/4 cup lime juice

1/4 cup olive or vegetable oil

2 tablespoons chopped fresh cilantro

2 tablespoons chopped onion

2 teaspoons chili powder

1 teaspoon ground cumin

1/2 teaspoon salt

1/4 teaspoon red pepper sauce

Mix all ingredients.

one serving: Calories 290 (Calories from Fat 180); Fat 20g; (Saturated 5g); Cholesterol 85mg; Sodium 210mg; Carbohydrate 1g (Dietary Fiber 0g); Protein 27g. % Daily Value: Vitamin A 2%; Vitamin C 2%; Calcium 2%; Iron 6%. Diet Exchanges: 4 Lean Meat. Carbohydrate Choices: 0

Adobe Pie

PREP: 20 MINUTES • BAKE: 19 MINUTES • 6 SERVINGS

1 pound ground beef

1 medium onion, chopped (1 cup)

1 can (14 1/2 ounces) diced tomatoes with roasted garlic, undrained

1 can (11 ounces) whole kernel corn with red and green peppers, drained

1/2 cup coarsely chopped pimiento-stuffed olives

1/3 cup raisins

2 teaspoons ground cumin

1/2 teaspoon ground cinnamon

1 pouch (6.5 ounces) golden corn bread and muffin mix

1/3 cup milk

2 tablespoons butter or margarine, melted

1 egg

1/4 cup canned diced green chiles

1/2 cup shredded Colby cheese

holiday FLAVOR *twist*

Would you like your Adobe Pie a little spicier? Use shredded pepper Monterey Jack cheese instead of the Colby and serve with a hot salsa.

1. Heat oven to 400°. Spray 2-quart casserole with cooking spray. Cook beef and onion in 12-inch skillet over medium heat, stirring occasionally, until brown, about 8 minutes; drain.

2. Stir in tomatoes, corn, olives, raisins, cumin and cinnamon. Spoon into casserole. Prepare corn bread as directed on pouch, using milk, margarine and egg; stir chiles and half of cheese into batter. Spread over beef mixture.

3. Bake uncovered 12 minutes. Sprinkle with remaining cheese. Bake 5 to 7 minutes or until corn bread is golden brown.

one serving: Calories 475 (Calories from Fat 225); Fat 25g; (Saturated 11g); Cholesterol 100mg; Sodium 950mg; Carbohydrate 44g (Dietary Fiber 5g); Protein 23g. % Daily Value: Vitamin A 16%; Vitamin C 14%; Calcium 16%; Iron 20%. Diet Exchanges: 2 1/2 Starch, 1 Vegetable, 2 Medium-Fat Meat, 2 Fat. Carbohydrate Choices: 3

Mexican Confetti Eggs

These pretty little eggs are like miniature piñatas—just break them open for instant fun!

HOW TO DO IT:

1. Punch a hole the size of a quarter in end of each egg. Drain out contents; rinse and let dry in egg carton.

2. Fill each egg half full with confetti. Cut 1-inch squares of tissue paper. Glue squares to egg shell, covering hole and entire egg. Glue on additional confetti to decorate outside of egg if desired.

3. Line basket with shredded paper. Place decorated eggs in basket. Crush eggs to release confetti.

WHAT YOU NEED:

Uncooked eggs in carton

Confetti

Assorted colored tissue paper

Craft glue

Basket, if desired

Shredded colored paper, if desired

Tres Leches Cake

PREP: 15 MINUTES • BAKE: 38 MINUTES • STAND: 5 MINUTES • CHILL: 3 HOURS •
15 SERVINGS

1 package (1 pound 2.25 ounces) yellow cake mix with pudding

1 cup water

1/3 cup vegetable oil

3 eggs

1 cup whipping (heavy) cream

1 cup whole milk

1 can (14 ounces) sweetened condensed milk

1/3 cup rum or 1 tablespoon rum extract plus enough water to measure 1/3 cup

1 cup whipping (heavy) cream

2 tablespoons rum or 1 teaspoon rum extract

1/2 teaspoon vanilla

1 cup flaked coconut, toasted

1/2 cup chopped pecans, toasted

holiday
FLAVOR *twist*

Don't have enough time to make this recipe all in one day? You can prepare it up through the baking in step 3 the night before. Make the rum-flavored whipped cream and spread over the cake just before serving

1. Heat oven to 350°. Grease bottom only of rectangular pan, 13 × 9 × 2 inches, with shortening.

2. Beat cake mix, water, oil and eggs in large bowl on low speed 30 seconds; beat on medium speed 2 minutes. Pour into pan.

3. Bake 33 to 38 minutes or until toothpick inserted in center comes out clean. Let stand 5 minutes. Pierce top of hot cake every 1/2 inch with long-tined fork, wiping fork occasionally to reduce sticking. Mix 1 cup whipping cream, the whole milk, sweetened condensed milk and 1/3 cup rum in large bowl. Carefully pour whipping cream mixture evenly over top of cake. Cover and refrigerate about 3 hours or until chilled and most of whipping cream mixture has been absorbed into cake.

4. Beat 1 cup whipping cream, 2 tablespoons rum and the vanilla in chilled large bowl with electric mixer on high speed until soft peaks form. Frost cake with whipped cream mixture. Sprinkle with coconut and pecans. Store covered in refrigerator.

one serving: Calories 490 (Calories from Fat 250); Fat 28g (Saturated 12g); Cholesterol 90mg; Sodium 330mg; Carbohydrate 52g (Dietary Fiber 1g); Protein 7g. % Daily Value: Vitamin A 10%; Vitamin C 0%; Calcium 18%; Iron 4%. Diet Exchanges: 2 Starch, 1 1/2 Other Carbohydrates, 5 1/2 Fat. Carbohydrate Choices: 3 1/2

MOTHER'S DAY

A DAY DEDICATED TO MOM has been a tradition in England since the early 1600s when "Mothering Sunday" was celebrated. In 1872 Julia Ward Howe (who also wrote the words to the "Battle Hymn of the Republic") suggested the holiday be recognized in America. The United States was recovering from the Civil War, and Howe hoped the day would promote peace and unity. In 1907, Anna Jarvis of Philadelphia took up Howe's crusade and—in response to Jarvis's vigorous campaign—President Woodrow Wilson, in 1914, declared the second Sunday in May to be Mother's Day. To show your love, give Mom a reprieve from her kitchen duties and prepare this extra-special brunch in her honor.

BRUNCH FOR MOM

SERVES 10

*Peachy Mimosas

*Smoked Salmon and Egg Wraps

Fresh Fruit Salad

*Cinnamon Streusel Coffee Cake

* RECIPE FOLLOWS

Peachy Mimosas

PREP: 5 MINUTES • 12 SERVINGS (2/3 CUP EACH)

2 cups orange juice, chilled

2 cups peach nectar, chilled

1 bottle (1 liter) regular or nonalcoholic dry champagne or sparkling wine, chilled

1. Mix orange juice and peach nectar in 1 1/2-quart pitcher.

2. Pour champagne into glasses until half full. Fill glasses with juice mixture.

one serving: Calories 100 (Calories from Fat 0); Fat 0g; (Saturated 0g); Cholesterol 0mg; Sodium 10mg; Carbohydrate 11g (Dietary Fiber 0g); Protein 1g. % Daily Value: Vitamin A 2%; Vitamin C 26%; Calcium 0%; Iron 2%. Diet Exchanges: 1 Fruit, 1 Fat. Carbohydrate Choices: 1

holiday DO-AHEAD *tip*

For the best flavor and punch, serve mimosas icy cold in frosty glasses. To frost, place glasses on a tray and freeze 1 hour or more until serving time.

holiday FLAVOR *twist*

Please mom by using her favorite juice or blend of juices. For example, use cranberry juice cocktail for the peach nectar, instead of blending juices, use 4 cups orange juice. Use whatever mom likes best. And don't forget the kids! Have a bottle of nonalcoholic sparkling beverage on hand so they can enjoy this pretty drink as well.

Smoked Salmon and Egg Wraps

PREP: 10 MINUTES • COOK: 10 MINUTES • BAKE: 10 MINUTES • 12 SERVINGS

12 eggs

2 tablespoons milk or water

1/2 teaspoon seasoned salt

1/4 cup chopped fresh or 1 tablespoon dried dill weed

12 flour tortillas (8 inches in diameter)

1 package (4 1/2 ounces) smoked salmon, broken into pieces

1/2 cup finely chopped red onion

1 1/2 cups shredded Havarti cheese (6 ounces)

Dill weed sprigs, if desired

holiday FLAVOR *twist*

Why not use flavored tortillas instead of plain flour tortillas? Not only do they add flavor, they also add extra color to the brunch table.

holiday DO-AHEAD *tip*

Make some time to enjoy a mimosa with your guests by preparing the wraps up to 2 hours ahead; cover with foil and refrigerate. To serve, bake about 13 to 15 minutes or until hot.

1. Heat oven to 350°. Line jelly roll pan, 15 1/2 × 10 1/2 × 1 inch, with aluminum foil. Beat eggs, milk and seasoned salt thoroughly with fork or wire whisk until a uniform yellow.

2. Spray 12-inch nonstick skillet with cooking spray. Pour egg mixture into skillet. As mixture begins to set at bottom and side, gently lift cooked portions with spatula so that thin, uncooked portion can flow to bottom. Avoid constant stirring. Cook 8 to 10 minutes or until eggs are thickened throughout but still moist. Stir in chopped dill weed.

3. Spoon about 1/3 cup eggs down center of each tortilla. Top with salmon, onion and cheese. Fold opposite sides of each tortilla over filling (sides will not meet in center). Roll up tortilla, beginning at one of the open ends. Place wraps, seam sides down, in pan. Cover with foil. Bake about 10 minutes or until cheese is melted. Garnish with dill weed sprigs.

one serving: Calories 280 (Calories from Fat 125); Fat 14g; (Saturated 6g); Cholesterol 230mg; Sodium 520mg; Carbohydrate 25g (Dietary Fiber 2g); Protein 15g. % Daily Value: Vitamin A 10%; Vitamin C 0%; Calcium 16%; Iron 12%. Diet Exchanges: 1 1/2 Starch, 2 Medium-Fat Meat. Carbohydrate Choices: 1 1/2

Mom's Mini-Frame and Candy Favor

Mom will love this special touch—pick a current photo, or pull one from her past, such as a wedding photo, high school graduation or any other photo that she would like. This is also a lovely gift for a woman who has been like a mother to you—perhaps an aunt, a close family friend or a mentor.

HOW TO DO IT:

1. Insert photo in picture frame.

2. Place candies on center of tulle; tie with ribbon. Place next to picture frame.

WHAT YOU NEED:

Photo of Mom

Mini picture frame

Assorted candies

8-inch square tulle or netting

1/4-inch-wide ribbon

Cinnamon Streusel Coffee Cake

PREP: 10 MINUTES • BAKE: 22 MINUTES • 10 SERVINGS

Streusel Topping (below)

2 cups Original Bisquick mix

2/3 cup milk or water

2 tablespoons sugar

1 egg

holiday *FLAVOR twist*

A vanilla drizzle will not only make this coffee cake look more special, it also adds an extra touch of flavor. Mix together 3/4 cup powdered sugar, about 1 tablespoon warm water and 1/4 teaspoon vanilla until smooth and thin enough to drizzle. Drizzle over the warm coffee cake.

1. Heat oven to 375°. Grease round pan, 9 × 1 1/2 inches. Make Streusel Topping; set aside.

2. Stir remaining ingredients until blended. Spread in pan. Sprinkle with topping.

3. Bake 18 to 22 minutes or until golden brown. Serve warm or cool.

Streusel Topping

1/3 cup Original Bisquick mix

1/3 cup packed brown sugar

1/2 teaspoon ground cinnamon

2 tablespoons firm butter or margarine

Mix Bisquick mix, brown sugar and cinnamon. Cut in butter, using fork or pastry blender, until mixture is crumbly.

one serving: 185 (Calories from Fat 65); Fat 7g; (Saturated 3g); Cholesterol 30mg; Sodium 430mg; Carbohydrate 27g (Dietary Fiber 0g); Protein 3g. % Daily Value: Vitamin A 2%; Vitamin C 0%; Calcium 8%; Iron 6%. Diet Exchanges: 1 Starch, 1 Other Carbohydrates, 1 Fat. Carbohydrate Choices: 2

Teacup Candle

Buy Mom a special teacup and saucer, and give it to her as a present. This simple project is just right for very small kids to make—however, remember to have an adult light the candle. To make this teacup candle extra special, place it on top of her favorite frosted layer cake.

WHAT YOU NEED:

Miniature or small teacup with saucer

Frosted 8- or 9-inch 2-layer cake

Small candle (can be floating candle)

Fresh flowers (such as pansies, begonias, nasturtiums, violets, roses, dianthus or carnations)

HOW TO DO IT:

1. Place candle inside teacup (with small amount of water if floating candle).

2. Arrange flowers around teacup.

3. Light the candle.

MEMORIAL DAY

MEMORIAL DAY AROSE FROM THE PRACTICE of decorating the graves of Confederate (Southern) and Union (Northern) soldiers shortly after the Civil War. A movement to honor soldiers of all wars grew out of that simple gesture and, in 1868, "Decoration Day" was widely recognized and observed on May 30. The name of the holiday was changed to Memorial Day in an effort to recognize not only soldiers who died fighting for their country, but deceased family members and friends as well. In 1971, the government officially fixed Memorial Day as the last Monday in May. Today, the custom of placing flowers and attending to the graves of loved ones continues. However you choose to observe the day, this "moveable feast," with its portable salads and sides, is ready when you are.

START THE SUMMER
SALAD PICNIC

SERVES 6–8

*Ranch Pretzel Nibblers

*Mandarin Chicken Salad

*Creamy Coleslaw

*Poppy Seed Fruit Salad

Breadsticks

*Fresh Mint Chocolate Chip Cookies

Grapes

Iced Tea

*RECIPE FOLLOWS

Ranch Pretzel Nibblers

PREP: 5 MINUTES • BAKE: 10 MINUTES • COOL: 30 MINUTES • 16 SERVINGS (1/2 CUP EACH)

1 package (14 ounces) sourdough pretzel nuggets (about 5 cups)

3 cups checkerboard-shape or tiny twist-shape pretzels

1/3 cup vegetable oil

1 envelope (1 ounce) ranch dressing mix

1. Heat oven to 325°. Place pretzels in ungreased jelly roll pan, 15 1/2 × 10 1/2 × 1 inch. Mix oil and dressing mix (dry) in small bowl. Pour over pretzels; stir to coat.

2. Bake 10 minutes, stirring once. Cool completely, about 30 minutes. Store tightly covered.

one serving: Calories 170 (Calories from Fat 55); Fat 6g; (Saturated 1g); Cholesterol 0mg; Sodium 980mg; Carbohydrate 76g (Dietary Fiber 1g); Protein 3g. % Daily Value: Vitamin A 0%; Vitamin C 0%; Calcium 0%; Iron 8%. Diet Exchanges: 1 1/2 Starch, 1 Fat. Carbohydrate Choices: 2

holiday
DO-AHEAD *tip*

Relax! You can make these tasty nibblers up to 1 month ahead of your picnic and store in a tightly covered container. Watch out—they make very tempting snacks!

Mandarin Chicken Salad

PREP 15 MINUTES • COOK: 5 MINUTES • 6 SERVINGS

2 tablespoons butter or margarine

1 package (3 oz) Oriental-flavor ramen noodle soup mix

2 tablespoons sesame seed

1/4 cup sugar

1/4 cup white vinegar

1 tablespoons sesame or vegetable oil

1/2 teaspoons pepper

2 cups cut-up cooked chicken

1/4 cup dry-roasted peanuts, if desired

4 medium green onions, sliced (1/4 cup)

1 bag (16 oz) coleslaw mix

1 can (11 oz) mandarin orange segments, drained

holiday
DO-AHEAD *tip*

If you're taking this salad on a picnic, toss everything except the noodle mixture and the dressing in a large portable container. Once you arrive, add noodle mixture and dressing, then cover and gently shake or spin to "toss."

1. Melt butter in 10-inch skillet over medium heat. Stir in seasoning packet from soup mix. Break block of noodles into bite-sized pieces over skillet; stir into butter mixture.

2. Cook noodles 2 minutes, stirring occasionally. Stir in sesame seed. Cook about 2 minutes longer, stirring occasionally, until noodles are golden brown; remove from heat.

3. Mix sugar, vinegar, oil and pepper in large bowl. Add noodle mixture and remaining ingredients; toss.

one serving: Calories 290 (Calories from Fat 125); Fat 14g (Saturated 5g); Cholesterol 50mg; Sodium 260mg; Carbohydrate 25g (Dietary Fiber 3g); Protein 17g. % Daily Value: Vitamin A 12%; Vitamin C 34%; Calcium 6%; Iron 10% Exchanges: 1 Starch, 2 Vegetable, 1 1/2 Medium-Fat Meat, 1 Fat. Carbohydrate Choices: 1 1/2

Creamy Coleslaw

PREP: 15 MINUTES • CHILL: 1 HOUR • 8 SERVINGS

1/2 cup sour cream

1/4 cup mayonnaise or salad dressing

1 tablespoon sugar

2 teaspoons lemon juice

2 teaspoons Dijon mustard

1/2 teaspoon celery seed

1/4 teaspoon pepper

1/2 medium head green cabbage, finely shredded or chopped (4 cups)

1 small carrot, shredded (1/2 cup)

1 small onion, chopped (1/4 cup)

holiday shortcut

Forget about shredding the cabbage and carrot. Instead pick up a package of cole-slaw mix in the produce department of the grocery store.

holiday FLAVOR twist

Toss in red grapes, crumbled blue cheese and toasted walnuts for extra-special flavor and crunch.

1. Mix all ingredients except cabbage, carrot and onion in large glass or plastic bowl. Add remaining ingredients; toss until evenly coated.

2. Cover and refrigerate at least 1 hour to blend flavors.

one serving: Calories 100 (Calories from Fat 70); Fat 8g; (Saturated 3g); Cholesterol 15mg; Sodium 90mg; Carbohydrate 7g (Dietary Fiber 2g); Protein 2g. % Daily Value: Vitamin A 26%; Vitamin C 32%; Calcium 4%; Iron 2%. Diet Exchanges: 1 Vegetable, 1 1/2 Fat. Carbohydrate Choices: 1/2

Art in the Park Picnic

Want a low-key way to keep the kids entertained? This is perfect. Plus, if the weather doesn't cooperate, this is an easy picnic to move inside—and all you'll be missing is the ants!

HOW TO DO IT:

1. Fill the sections of a plastic art bin with fabric markers, artist palette knives—which make great cheese spreaders—and your favorite picnic foods.

2. Place large canvas on flat, grassy area. If using the smaller pieces, place them in a circle. Be sure that there is space for everyone.

3. Put plastic art bin in the center of the canvas.

4. Create your favorite designs on the canvas using the markers while enjoying your snack foods.

WHAT YOU NEED:

1 plastic art bin or case

Fabric markers

Artist palette knives

Assortment of picnic foods (sandwiches, cheese, dips, chips, olives, or other purchased gourmet foods)

1 piece large canvas or muslin or smaller pieces

Poppy Seed Fruit Salad

PREP: 15 MINUTES • 8 SERVINGS

1/4 cup honey

1/4 cup frozen (thawed) limeade concentrate

2 teaspoons poppy seed

1 cup strawberries, cut in half

1 cup cubed pineapple

1 cup fresh blueberries

1 cup cubed watermelon

1/4 cup slivered almonds, toasted, if desired

holiday *FLAVOR twist*

You can use any kind of fresh fruit that you like in this salad. Try cantaloupe, raspberries, honeydew melon, kiwifruit, grapes or oranges or whatever is in season.

holiday *shortcut*

To save time washing and cutting up fruit, purchase packaged cut-up fresh fruit from the produce department of the grocery store. You will need about 4 cups.

1. Mix honey, limeade concentrate and poppy seed in medium bowl.

2. Carefully toss fruit with honey mixture. Sprinkle with almonds.

one serving: Calories 95 (Calories from Fat 10); Fat 1g; (Saturated 0g); Cholesterol 0mg; Sodium 0mg; Carbohydrate 21g (Dietary Fiber 1g); Protein 0g. % Daily Value: Vitamin A 2%; Vitamin C 32%; Calcium 0%; Iron 0%. Diet Exchanges: 1 1/2 Fruit. Carbohydrate Choices: 1 1/2

Fresh Mint Chocolate Chip Cookies

PREP: 15 MINUTES • BAKE: 13 MINUTES PER SHEET • ABOUT 3 1/2 DOZEN COOKIES

1 1/3 cups sugar

3/4 cup butter or margarine, softened

1 tablespoon finely chopped fresh mint leaves

1 egg

2 cups all-purpose flour

1 teaspoon baking soda

1 teaspoon salt

1 package (10 ounces) mint-chocolate chips (1 1/2 cups)

holiday shortcut

The fresh chopped mint adds a lovely flavor, but if you don't have time, use 1/4 teaspoon mint extract instead.

holiday FLAVOR twist

Want another summery version of this all-time favorite cookie? Substitute raspberry chocolate chips for the mint chips.

1. Heat oven to 350°. Beat sugar, butter, mint and egg in large bowl with electric mixer on medium speed, or mix with spoon. Stir in flour, baking soda and salt. Stir in chocolate chips.

2. Drop dough by rounded tablespoonfuls about 2 inches apart onto ungreased cookie sheet. Bake 11 to 13 minutes or until golden brown. Cool 1 to 2 minutes; remove from cookie sheet to wire rack.

one cookie: Calories 120 (Calories from Fat 55); Fat 6g; (Saturated 3g); Cholesterol 15mg; Sodium 80mg; Carbohydrate 15g (Dietary Fiber 0g); Protein 1g. % Daily Value: Vitamin A 2%; Vitamin C 0%; Calcium 0%; Iron 2%. Diet Exchanges: 1/2 Starch, 1/2 Other Carbohydrates, 1 Fat. Carbohydrate Choices: 1

Saturday Morning Breakfast Picnic

Have a busy Memorial Day weekend planned? This on-the-go morning picnic fits into the busiest schedule. And it's fun to have a morning picnic for a change. Try it any weekend you have a lot on your plate!

WHAT YOU NEED:

1 small produce crate

Assortment of breakfast foods (muffins, bagels, oranges, bananas, milk boxes, juice boxes, Thermos of coffee)

1 large kitchen towel

Thermos of coffee

HOW TO DO IT:

1. Fill produce crate with your favorite assortment of breakfast foods.

2. Wrap the crate in a kitchen towel. The towel can be used as a handle to carry your breakfast to the picnic spot, and once you're there, use it as a tablecloth.

3. After enjoying the picnic, clean up is a snap, using the kitchen towel.

FATHER'S DAY

A DAY SET ASIDE TO HONOR DEAR OLD DAD was the brainchild of Mrs. John B. Dodd, and Father's Day was first celebrated on June 19, 1910, in Spokane, Washington. Even though government officials in the state of Washington were quick to recognize the holiday's importance, it wasn't until 1966 that the president declared the third Sunday in June a U.S. holiday. There are numerous ways to pay tribute to Dad, so don't be afraid to break out of the "shirt-and-tie-gift" box. Good food and a little wait service can go a long way to showing Pop how much you care. This delicious menu is a nice way to encourage Dad to put his feet up and enjoy himself.

BARBECUE FOR DAD

SERVES 5

Beer and Soda

*Savory Cheese Potatoes

*Beer Can Chicken

*Seven-Layer Salad

*Grilled Garlic Bread with Rosemary

Sundaes

*RECIPE FOLLOWS

Savory Cheese Potatoes

PREP: 5 MINUTES • GRILL: 25 MINUTES • 5 SERVINGS

4 cups frozen O'Brien potatoes (from 28-ounce bag)

1/2 cup ranch dressing

1 cup shredded Cheddar and American cheese blend (4 ounces)

2 tablespoons grated Parmesan cheese

1. Heat coals or gas grill for direct heat. Cut 18 × 18-inch piece of heavy-duty aluminum foil. Spray with cooking spray. Place potatoes on center of foil. Drizzle with dressing; mix gently. Sprinkle with shredded cheese blend.

2. Fold foil over potatoes so edges meet. Seal edges, making tight 1/2-inch fold; fold again. Allow space on sides for circulation and expansion.

3. Cover and grill packets 4 to 5 inches from medium heat 20 to 25 minutes or until potatoes are tender. Place packet on serving platter. Cut large X across top of packet; fold back foil. Sprinkle with Parmesan cheese.

one serving: Calories 350 (Calories from Fat 170); Fat 19g; (Saturated 6g); Cholesterol 35mg; Sodium 870mg; Carbohydrate 35g (Dietary Fiber 3g); Protein 10g. % Daily Value: Vitamin A 6%; Vitamin C 10%; Calcium 20%; Iron 4%. Diet Exchanges: 2 Starch, 1 Vegetable, 3 1/2 Fat. Carbohydrate Choices: 2

holiday shortcut

If you like, you can prepare these potatoes in a disposable foil pan that can be purchased at the grocery store. Make the potatoes in the pan and cover with foil, then grill as directed.

Beer Can Chicken

PREP: 10 MINUTES • GRILL: 1 HOUR 30 MINUTES • STAND: 15 MINUTES • 6 SERVINGS

Basic Barbecue Rub (below)

4- to 4 1/2-pound whole broiler-fryer chicken

1 can (12 ounces) beer

holiday
FLAVOR *twist*

It's a family barbecue and you prefer not to use beer? No problem—just use a 12-ounce can of lemon-lime soda instead.

1. If using charcoal grill, place drip pan directly under grilling area, and arrange coals around edge of firebox. Heat coals or gas grill for indirect heat.

2. Make Basic Barbecue Rub. Fold wings of chicken across back with tips touching. Sprinkle rub inside cavity and all over outside of chicken; rub with fingers.

3. Pour 1/2 cup of beer from can. Hold chicken upright, with opening of body cavity down; insert beer can into cavity. Insert barbecue meat thermometer so tip is in thickest part of inside thigh muscle and does not touch bone.

4. Cover and grill chicken upright over drip pan or over unheated side of gas grill 4 to 6 inches from medium heat 1 hour 15 minutes to 1 hour 30 minutes or until thermometer reads 180° and juice is no longer pink when center of thigh is cut.

5. Using tongs, carefully lift chicken to rectangular pan, 13 × 9 × 2 inches, holding large metal spatula under beer can for support. Let stand 15 minutes before carving. Remove beer can; discard.

Basic Barbecue Rub

1 tablespoon paprika

2 teaspoons salt

1/2 teaspoon garlic powder

1/2 teaspoon onion powder

1/2 teaspoon pepper

Mix all ingredients.

one serving: Calories 315 (Calories from Fat 160); Fat 18g; (Saturated 5g); Cholesterol 115mg; Sodium 890mg; Carbohydrate 3g (Dietary Fiber 0g); Protein 35g. % Daily Value: Vitamin A 16%; Vitamin C 0%; Calcium 2%; Iron 10%. Diet Exchanges: 5 Lean Meat, 1 Fat. Carbohydrate Choices: 0

Seven-Layer Salad

PREP: 25 MINUTES • CHILL: 2 HOURS • 6 SERVINGS

6 cups bite-size pieces mixed salad greens

2 medium stalks celery, thinly sliced (1 cup)

1 cup thinly sliced radishes

8 medium green onion, sliced (1/2 cup)

12 slices bacon, crisply cooked and crumbled

1 package (10 ounces) frozen green peas, thawed and drained

1 1/2 cups mayonnaise or salad dressing

1/2 cup grated Parmesan cheese or shredded Cheddar cheese (2 ounces)

holiday shortcut

No time to cook the bacon? No problem, just buy bacon bits from the spice section of your supermarket.

1. Place salad greens in large glass bowl. Layer celery, radishes, onions, bacon and peas on salad greens.

2. Spread mayonnaise over peas, covering top completely and sealing to edge of bowl. Sprinkle with cheese. Cover and refrigerate at least 2 hours to blend flavors but no longer than 12 hours. Toss before serving if desired. Store covered in refrigerator.

one serving: Calories 550 (Calories from fat 475); Fat 53g; (Saturdated 10g); Cholesterol 50mg; Sodium 740mg; Carbohydrate 12g (Dietary Fiber 5g); Protein 12g. % Daily Value: Vitamin A 44%; Vitamin C 38%; Calcium 18%; Iron 12%. Diet Exchanges: 2 Vegetable, 1 High-Fat Meat, 9 Fat. Carbohydrate Choices: 1

Mason Jar Candle

Shed some light on your Father's Day barbecue! These candleholders will tickle Dad and are a great project for the littlest kids. Just be sure to ask an older child or a grown up to light the candle.

HOW TO DO IT:

1. Fill jar 1/2 full with marbles. Add water to just above marbles.

2. Place candle in center of jar, pushing candle down into marbles to bottom of jar.

3. Light candle with matches. Carefully pull up candle as it burns down to water level. (Blow out candle first, then relight.)

WHAT YOU NEED:

1-quart mason jar

1 to 2 cups clear or colored marbles

4- to 5-inch candle

Water

Matches

Grilled Garlic Bread with Rosemary

PREP: 10 MINUTES • GRILL: 15 MINUTES • 12 SERVINGS (1 SLICE EACH)

1 loaf (1 pound) unsliced French bread

1/2 cup butter or margarine, softened

2 tablespoons chopped fresh or 2 teaspoons dried rosemary leaves

1 tablespoon chopped fresh parsley or 1 teaspoon parsley flakes

1/4 to 1/2 teaspoon garlic powder

holiday FLAVOR twist

If Dad doesn't care for the strong flavor of rosemary, use chopped basil mixed with the parsley—it's milder and should be more to his liking.

Would you rather bake, not grill, this bread? Then heat the oven to 400° and prepare bread as directed in the recipe. Wrap the bread in aluminum foil, and bake about 15 minutes or until hot. It's just as delicious, and frees up the grill.

1. Heat coals or gas grill for direct heat. Cut bread loaf into 1-inch slices without cutting through bottom of loaf. Mix remaining ingredients; spread on both sides of bread slices. Wrap bread loaf in heavy-duty aluminum foil.

2. Cover and grill bread 5 to 6 inches from medium heat 10 to 15 minutes, turning once, until hot.

one serving: Calories 165 (Calories from Fat 80); Fat 9g; (Saturated 5g); Cholesterol 20mg; Sodium 270mg; Carbohydrate 19g (Dietary Fiber 1g); Protein 3g. % Daily Value: Vitamin A 6%; Vitamin C 0%; Calcium 2%; Iron 6%. Diet Exchanges: 1 Starch, 1 Fat. Carbohydrate Choices: 1

Hanging Flower Vase

Who said Mom gets all the flowers? Dad will love getting these flowers, and they work well with the Mason Jar Candles (page 111). The candles and the flower vases use simple items—you may have everything you need at home, with no shopping. And while this is a very kid-friendly project, just as with lighting the candles—don't ask the little ones to bend the wire hanger—that's a job for older kids, or for Mom.

WHAT YOU NEED:

Wire coat hanger

1 1/2-pint mason jar

Ribbon or string

Water

Fresh flowers

HOW TO DO IT:

1. Holding hanger at top center just beneath hook, pull down at bottom center until hanger is straight.

2. Bend bottom 3 inches of hanger to 90-degree angle; bend and open into circle to fit neck of jar.

3. Place hanger around neck of jar to hold firmly. Tie string around base of hanger to secure.

4. Fill jar 1/2 full with water; arrange flowers in vase. Tie ribbon around neck of jar, and make a bow. Hang using hook of wire hanger.

INDEPENDENCE DAY

HAPPY BIRTHDAY TO US! Independence Day, or the Fourth of July, as it is commonly called, marks the day in 1776 when our founding forefathers signed the Declaration of Independence. As its title implies, the Declaration stated that the United States of America was no longer a colony of England and officially declared our independence as a country. As early as 1777, we proudly showed off our stars and stripes with lots of noise—from clanging bells to booming cannons. By the 1800s, parades, picnics and fireworks were a tradition in our countrywide patriotic party. This simple but tasty meal is a wonderful prelude to a night of fireworks-watching "oohing" and "aahing."

CELEBRATE THE 4TH

SERVES 8

Lemonade

*Honey Lime Fruit Salad

*Sour Cream and Onion Burgers

Grilled Hot Dogs

Bread Sticks

*Spicy Grilled Corn

*Three-Bean Bacon Medley

*Flag Cake

*RECIPE FOLLOWS

Clay Pot Condiment Servers

Add extra fun to this holiday meal and put your burger "fixin's" in attractive clay pots.

HOW TO DO IT:

1. Turn large pot upside down; place saucer on top. Line saucer with plastic wrap; fill with burger toppings

2. Line small pot with plastic wrap and set upright; fill with breadsticks.

3. Line small saucer with plastic wrap; fill with pickles and olives.

WHAT YOU NEED:

1 large terra-cotta pot with saucer (8 to 10 inches in diameter)

Colored plastic wrap

Burger toppings, condiments or relishes (sliced tomatoes and onions)

1 small terra-cotta pot with saucer (4 to 6 inches in diameter)

Breadsticks

Pickles and olives

Honey Lime Fruit Salad

PREP: 10 MINUTES • 8 SERVINGS

1/2 cup honey

1/2 cup frozen (thawed) limeade concentrate

1 tablespoon poppy seed, if desired

8 cups cut-up fresh fruit

1/2 cup slivered almonds, toasted

holiday FLAVOR *twist*

Not only is this pretty—it's delicious as well. Cut watermelon into 3- to 4-inch wedges, about 1/2 inch thick. Place wedges (points facing out) around the edge of large platter, stacking into 3 to 4 layers. Place the fruit salad in center, and garnish with sprigs of mint.

1. Mix honey, limeade concentrate and poppy seed in large bowl.

2. Carefully toss fruit with honey mixture. Sprinkle with almonds.

one serving: Calories 220 (Calories from Fat 45); Fat 5g; (Saturated 1g); Cholesterol 0mg; Sodium 5mg; Carbohydrate 45g (Dietary Fiber 4g); Protein 3g. % Daily Value: Vitamin A 22%; Vitamin C 88%; Calcium 4%; Iron 4%. Diet Exchanges: 3 Fruit, 1 Fat. Carbohydrate Choices: 3

Sour Cream and Onion Burgers

PREP: 10 MINUTES • GRILL: 15 MINUTES • 8 SANDWICHES

2 pounds ground beef

1 envelope (about 1 1/2 ounces) onion soup mix

1 cup sour cream

1/2 cup dry bread crumbs

1/8 teaspoon pepper

8 sandwich buns, split,

Leaf lettuce, if desired

holiday
FLAVOR *twist*

Want some independence from the usual burger and bun? Serve the burgers on focaccia. Use 1 round focaccia bread (about 10 inches in diameter), cut horizontally in half, then cut into 8 wedges.

1. Heat coals or gas grill for direct heat. Mix all ingredients except buns and lettuce. Shape mixture into 8 patties, about 1/2 inch thick.

2. Cover and grill patties 4 to 6 inches from medium heat 10 to 15 minutes, turning once, until patties are no longer pink in center and juice is clear. Serve with lettuce in buns.

one sandwich: Calories 435 (Calories from Fat 215); Fat 24g; (Saturated 10g); Cholesterol 85mg; Sodium 670mg; Carbohydrate 31g (Dietary Fiber 2g); Protein 26g. % Daily Value: Vitamin A 4%; Vitamin C 0%; Calcium 12%; Iron 20%. Diet Exchanges: 2 Starch, 3 Medium-Fat Meat, 1 Fat. Carbohydrate Choices: 2

Spicy Grilled Corn

PREP: 15 MINUTES • GRILL: 30 MINUTES • 12 SERVINGS

1/3 cup butter or margarine, softened

3 tablespoons taco seasoning mix
(from 1.25-ounce envelope)

12 ears corn with husks

holiday FLAVOR *twist*

Who doesn't love tender, sweet corn at a 4th of July meal? For the best flavor, buy corn the day you plan to serve it; keep it cold until you're ready to cook it.

holiday *shortcut*

If the corn and burgers don't all fit on your grill, there are two things you can do. You can grill the corn first and then cook the burgers—or make the corn in the microwave. Husk the corn, and place each ear on microwave-safe plastic wrap or waxed paper. Brush the corn with the butter mixture, then wrap. Microwave 4 ears of corn 6 to 8 minutes, turning once. Let stand 2 minutes. Repeat with remaining corn.

1. Heat coals or gas grill for direct heat. Mix butter and taco seasoning mix. Carefully pull back husk of each ear of corn; remove silk. Spread butter mixture over corn. Pull husks back over ears; tie husks securely with thin piece of husk or string.

2. Grill corn uncovered 4 to 6 inches from medium heat 20 to 30 minutes, turning frequently, until tender.

one serving: Calories 165 (Calories from Fat 55); Fat 6g; (Saturated 3g); Cholesterol 15mg; Sodium 170mg; Carbohydrate 27g (Dietary Fiber 3g); Protein 4g. % Daily Value: Vitamin A 12%; Vitamin C 6%; Calcium 0%; Iron 4%. Diet Exchanges: 1 1/2 Starch, 1 Fat. Carbohydrate Choices: 2

Three-Bean Bacon Medley

COOK: 10 MINUTES • 8 SERVINGS (1/2 CUP EACH)

1 quart deli three-bean salad (4 cups)

2 tablespoons packed brown sugar

8 slices bacon, crisply cooked and crumbled

1. Heat three-bean salad and brown sugar in 2-quart saucepan over medium-high heat, stirring frequently, about 10 minutes, until hot and sugar is dissolved.

2. Sprinkle with bacon.

one serving: Calories 190 (Calories from Fat 135); Fat 15g; (Saturated 3g); Cholesterol 5mg; Sodium 360mg; Carbohydrate 11g (Dietary Fiber 2g); Protein 4g. % Daily Value: Vitamin A 4%; Vitamin C 2%; Calcium 2%; Iron 6%. Diet Exchanges: 1 Starch, 3 Fat. Carbohydrate Choices: 1

holiday
FLAVOR *twist*

You can often find three-bean salad in the deli case in the summer because it's perfect for picnics. However, if you can't find it, use two 15-ounce cans of three-bean salad, undrained, instead.

Flag Cake

PREP: 15 MINUTES • BAKE: 35 MINUTES • COOL: 1 HOUR 10 MINUTES • 15 SERVINGS

1 package (1 pound 2.25 ounces) yellow cake mix with pudding

1 1/4 cups water

1/3 cup vegetable oil

3 eggs

1 tub (16 ounces) vanilla frosting or 1 tub (12 ounces) vanilla whipped ready-to-spread frosting

1/3 cup blueberries

1 pint (2 cups) strawberries, stems removed and strawberries cut in half

holiday FLAVOR twist

This patriotic cake is so simple and so versatile! Feel free to use any flavor of cake mix in this recipe—just follow the package directions. To make this cake easy to take, you can frost and decorate it right in the pan.

1. Heat oven to 350°. Grease bottom only of rectangular pan, 13 × 9 × 2 inches, with shortening. Make cake mix as directed on package, using water, oil and eggs. Pour into pan.

2. Bake 30 to 35 minutes or until toothpick inserted in center comes out clean. Cool 10 minutes. Run knife around sides of pan to loosen cake; remove from pan to wire rack. Cool completely, about 1 hour.

3. Frost top and sides of cake with frosting. For flag design, arrange blueberries on upper left corner of frosted cake to create stars; arrange strawberries in rows over frosted cake to create stripes. Serve immediately. Store covered in refrigerator.

one serving: Calories 345 (Calories from Fat 125); Fat 14g; (Saturated 6g); Cholesterol 45mg; Sodium 250mg; Carbohydrate 52g (Dietary Fiber 1g); Protein 3g. % Daily Value: Vitamin A 0%; Vitamin C 10%; Calcium 4%; Iron 4%. Diet Exchanges: 1 Starch, 2 1/2 Other Carbohydrates, 2 1/2 Fat. Carbohydrate Choices: 3 1/2

Flower Plates

Bring summer's beautiful flowers directly on to your plates with these pretty serving plates. Pick flowers from your garden, or look at the farmer's market for the best of summer's floral bounty. These look terrific teamed with the Clay Condiment Servers (page 117). It's also a pretty way way to serve fresh fruit or cheese slices for the burgers.

WHAT YOU NEED:

Fresh flower petals

Serving plate (maximum of 10 inches in diameter)

Clear plastic wrap (cling type)

Sliced fruit or cheese

HOW TO DO IT:

1. Arrange petals on plate.

2. Stretch plastic wrap over plate, making sure surface is tight and flat.

3. Arrange fruit on surface of plastic wrap so petals show through.

LABOR DAY

IN 1882, A NEW YORK CITY UNION LEADER, wanting to designate a day to honor working people, conceived of Labor Day. Today, most view the first Monday in September as a sign of summer's end. Labor Day, officially recognized as a holiday in 1894, usually begins a period of shorter, darker days, cooler temps and no-nonsense back-to-work-and-school attitudes. And, while a clambake is a wonderful way to say farewell to the season, unfortunately not everyone has access to the beach—hence this seaside-inspired menu that can be enjoyed anywhere. While it's not possible to stop summer from winding down, it *is* possible to make every last minute count.

SEASIDE BASH
IN THE BACKYARD

SERVES 8

Bloody Marys or Tomato Juice

*Seafaring Packets

*Hummus and Olive Tapenade Spread

Crackers

Crudite

*Lemonade Tea

*Focaccia with Grilled Garlic

*Quick Fruit Cobbler

*RECIPE FOLLOWS

Kid's "Go Fish" Party Dishes

Nothing fishy about how fun—and easy—these party dishes are to make. Let the kids go wild with the stickers—and be fair, let the adults go crazy too!

HOW TO DO IT:

1. Decorate cups with stickers.

2. Place unfolded napkin (pattern side up) in each strawberry crate; fold back napkin edges. Fill crate with crackers and candies. Fill cups with fruit drink.

WHAT YOU NEED:

Plastic cups

Stickers

5-inch paper napkins

Green plastic strawberry crates

Fish-shaped crackers

Fish-shaped candies

Any flavored fruit drink

Seafaring Packets

PREP: 20 MINUTES • GRILL: 20 MINUTES • 8 SERVINGS

32 clams in shells (littleneck or cherrystones) (about 2 1/2 pounds)

32 uncooked medium shrimp in shells, thawed if frozen (about 1 1/4 pounds))

32 sea scallops (about 2 1/2 pounds)

8 ears corn, husked and cut into fourths

32 large cherry tomatoes

Lemon Butter (below) or Chive Butter (below)

Fresh chive stems or chopped fresh chives, if desired

holiday FLAVOR *twist*

Use mussels if clams aren't available or you prefer mussels over clams. If someone doesn't care for either clams or mussels, just double the amount of shrimp or scallops instead.

1. Heat coals or gas grill for direct heat. Place clams, shrimp, scallops, corn and tomatoes on one side of eight 8 × 12-inch sheet of heavy-duty aluminum foil. Drizzle 1 tablespoon of either Lemon Butter or Chive Butter over seafood and vegetables on each sheet.

2. Fold foil over seafood and vegetables so edges meet. Seal edges, making tight 1/2-inch fold; fold again. Allow space on sides for circulation and expansion.

3. Cover and grill packets 4 to 5 inches from medium heat 15 to 20 minutes or until clams open, shrimp are pink and firm and vegetables are tender.* Place packets on plates. Cut large × across top of each packet; fold back foil. Top with chives.

Lemon Butter

1/2 cup butter or margarine, melted

1 tablespoon grated lemon peel

Mix ingredients.

Chive Butter

1/2 cup butter or margarine, melted

1 tablespoon chopped fresh or 1 teaspoon freeze-dried chives

Mix ingredients.

*Cooking time may vary depending on ingredients selected.

one serving: Calories 390 (Calories from Fat 135); Fat 15g; (Saturated 8g); Cholesterol 110mg; Sodium 360mg; Carbohydrate 32g (Dietary Fiber 4g); Protein 32g. % Daily Value: Vitamin A 30%; Vitamin C 22%; Calcium 12%; Iron 66%. Diet Exchanges: 2 Starch, 3 1/2 Lean Meat, 1 Fat. Carbohydrate Choices: 2

Hummus and Olive Tapenade Spread

PREP: 5 MINUTES • 20 SERVINGS (1 TABLESPOON EACH)

2 containers (7 ounces each) regular or roasted red pepper hummus

1 can (4 1/4 ounces) chopped ripe olives, drained

2 tablespoons Greek vinaigrette or zesty Italian dressing

1/8 teaspoon garlic powder

Chopped fresh parsley, if desired

Pita bread wedges or assorted crackers, if desired

holiday FLAVOR twist

You can substitute 3/4 cup chopped Kalamata olives for the ripe olives. Look for already-pitted Kalamata olives to save a little time.

holiday shortcut

Want an easy way to decorate this zesty spread? Reserve a little of the hummus for decorating with fun dots or swirls. You can put the extra hummus in a squeeze bottle or in a resealable plastic food-storage bag with a 1/8-inch opening cut from one corner.

1. Spread hummus on 8- to 10-inch serving plate.

2. Mix olives, vinaigrette and garlic powder. Spread over hummus, leaving about 2-inch border of hummus around edge. Sprinkle with parsley. Serve with pita bread wedges.

one serving: Calories 20 (Calories from Fat 10); Fat 1g; (Saturated 0g); Cholesterol 0mg; Sodium 65mg; Carbohydrate 2g (Dietary Fiber 1g); Protein 1g. % Daily Value: Vitamin A 0%; Vitamin C 0%; Calcium 0%; Iron 2%. Diet Exchanges: one serving is free. Carbohydrate Choices: 0

Lemonade Tea

PREP: 5 MINUTES • 20 SERVINGS (1 CUP EACH)

2 cans (12 ounces each) frozen lemonade concentrate, thawed

3 quarts iced tea

holiday FLAVOR *twist*

With all the different flavors of tea available, you can give this lemonade tea a twist anytime. Try mint- or raspberry-flavored tea, English breakfast tea or green tea. For flavorful fun, float thin slices of lemon in serving glasses and then garnish with mint leaves.

1. Make lemonade as directed on can in 2-gallon beverage container.

2. Stir in tea. Serve over ice.

one serving: Calories 85 (Calories from Fat 0); Fat 0g; (Saturated 0g); Cholesterol 0mg; Sodium 5mg; Carbohydrate 21g (Dietary Fiber 0g); Protein 0g. % Daily Value: Vitamin A 0%; Vitamin C 14%; Calcium 0%; Iron 2%. Diet Exchanges: 1 1/2 Other Carbohydrates. Carbohydrate Choices: 1 1/2

Focaccia with Grilled Garlic

PREP: 5 MINUTES • GRILL: 35 MINUTES • 6 SERVINGS

2 large bulbs garlic

1 tablespoon olive or vegetable oil

1 teaspoon chopped fresh or 1/4 teaspoon dried thyme leaves

1 round focaccia bread, 12 inches in diameter (16 ounces)

1. Heat coals or gas grill. Peel loose paper-like layers from garlic bulbs, but do not separate cloves. Place each garlic bulb on 12-inch square of heavy-duty aluminum foil. Brush with oil; sprinkle with thyme. Wrap bulbs securely in foil.

2. Cover and grill garlic 4 to 6 inches from medium heat 25 to 35 minutes or until garlic cloves are very soft. Add focaccia to side of grill for last 8 to 10 minutes of grilling, turning once, until golden brown. To serve, squeeze garlic out of individual cloves onto slices of focaccia.

one serving: Calories 250 (Calories from Fat 80); Fat 9g; (Saturated 1g); Cholesterol 0mg; Sodium 630mg; Carbohydrate 37g (Dietary Fiber 1g); Protein 5g. % Daily Value: Vitamin A 0%; Vitamin C 0%; Calcium 0%; Iron 12%. Diet Exchanges: 2 Starch, 1 Other Carbohydrates, 1 1/2 Fat. Carbohydrate Choices: 2 1/2

holiday FLAVOR *twist*

Use two 8-inch focaccias or Italian bread shells instead of the 12-inch focaccia. Or squeeze the warm roasted garlic over slices of French bread.

Quick Fruit Cobbler

PREP: 10 MINUTES • BAKE: 20 MINUTES • 6 SERVINGS

1 can (21 ounces) fruit pie filling (any flavor)

1 cup Original Bisquick mix

1/4 cup milk

1 tablespoon sugar

1 tablespoon butter or margarine, softened

Whipped topping, if desired

holiday
FLAVOR *twist*

For a *fresh berry cobbler*, use 3 cups fresh berries (blueberries, raspberries, sliced strawberries) instead of the canned fruit. Add sugar to taste to the berries and about 3/4 cup water. Continue as directed.

1. Spread pie filling in ungreased 1 1/2-quart casserole. Place in cold oven. Heat oven to 400°; let heat 10 minutes. Remove casserole from oven.

2. While pie filling is heating, stir remaining ingredients until soft dough forms. Drop dough by 6 spoonfuls onto warm pie filling. Sprinkle with additional sugar if desired.

3. Bake 18 to 20 minutes or until topping is golden brown. Serve with whipped topping.

one serving: Calories 200 (Calories from Fat 45); Fat 5g; (Saturated 2g); Cholesterol 5mg; Sodium 300mg; Carbohydrate 38g (Dietary Fiber 1g); Protein 2g. % Daily Value: Vitamin A 2%; Vitamin C 0%; Calcium 4%; Iron 4%. Diet Exchanges: 1 Starch, 1 1/2 Fruit, 1 Fat. Carbohydrate Choices: 2 1/2

HALLOWEEN

YEARS AGO, THE CELTS BELIEVED that witches and ghosts roamed the earth on the night of October 31, revisiting places they had inhabited when they were alive. In order to protect themselves and frighten off the evil creatures, the Celts wore masks when they ventured outdoors. These days, it seems almost the reverse is true: lively little children don masks and scary costumes to frighten each other as they scamper door to door soliciting tricks and treats from neighbors. However you define scary, chances are you'll find the following menus frightfully good.

HALLOWEEN FAMILY DINNER

SERVES 6

*Peanutty Pear Salad

*Ghostly Shepherd's Pie

Breadsticks

*Scarecrow Cake

Chocolate Milk

*RECIPE FOLLOWS

Peanutty Pear Salad

PREP: 10 MINUTES • 6 SERVINGS

Soy Dijon Vinaigrette (below)

6 cups bite-size pieces mixed salad greens

2 large or 3 medium unpeeled ripe pears, sliced

1/3 cup dry-roasted peanuts

1/3 cup golden raisins

1. Make Soy Dijon Vinaigrette

2. Divide salad greens among 6 plates. Top with pears, peanuts and raisins. Drizzle with vinaigrette. Serve immediately.

Soy Dijon Vinaigrette

2 tablespoons olive or vegetable oil

1 tablespoon lemon juice

2 teaspoons sugar

2 teaspoons soy sauce

1 teaspoon Dijon mustard

Shake all ingredients in tightly covered container.

one serving: Calories 185 (Calories from Fat 80); Fat 9g; (Saturated 1g); Cholesterol 0mg; Sodium 200mg; Carbohydrate 22g (Dietary Fiber 4g); Protein 4g. % Daily Value: Vitamin A 34%; Vitamin C 22%; Calcium 4%; Iron 6%. Diet Exchanges: 1 Fruit, 2 Vegetable, 1 1/2 Fat. Carbohydrate Choices: 1 1/2

holiday FLAVOR *twist*

A sweet variety of eating apple can be substituted for the pears, and regular raisins or dried cranberries can be used instead of golden raisins.

Ghostly Shepherd's Pie

PREP: 30 MINUTES • BAKE: 25 MINUTES • 6 SERVINGS

1 lb lean ground beef

1 medium onion, coarsely chopped

2 1/2 cups frozen mixed vegetables

1 can (14 1/2 oz) diced tomatoes with Italian herbs, undrained

1 jar (12 oz) home-style beef gravy

1 3/4 cups water

2 tablespoons butter or margarine

1/4 teaspoon garlic powder

1/2 cup milk

2 1/4 cups instant mashed potatoes

1/4 cup grated Parmesan cheese

1 egg, slightly beaten

holiday history

The early Celts believed you could drive away the ghosts that came out on Halloween by lighting lanterns or candles. Why not keep these little ghosts at bay by lighting candles at the dinner table?

1. Heat oven to 375°. Spray 12-inch skillet with cooking spray. Cook beef and onion over medium heat 8 to 10 minutes, stirring occasionally, until brown; drain.

2. Set 12 peas aside for garnish. Add remaining frozen vegetables, tomatoes and gravy to beef mixture. Heat to boiling; reduce heat to medium-low. Cover and cook 8 to 10 minutes, stirring occasionally, or until vegetables are crisp-tender.

3. Meanwhile, in medium saucepan, bring water, margarine and garlic powder to a boil. Remove from heat; add milk. Stir in potato flakes and cheese. Add egg; blend well.

4. Spoon ground beef mixture into ungreased 8-inch square (2-quart) or oval (2 1/2-quart) glass baking dish. With large spoon, make 6 mounds of potato mixture on top of beef mixture to resemble ghosts. Place 2 reserved peas on each mound to resemble eyes.

5. Bake at 375° for 20 to 25 minutes or until potatoes are set and mixture is thoroughly heated.

one serving: Calories 365 (Calories from Fat 170); Fat 19g (Saturated 9g); Cholesterol 95mg; Sodium 620mg; Carbohydrate 25g (Dietary Fiber 4g); Protein 23g. % Daily Value: Vitamin A 34%; Vitamin C 32%; Calcium 14%; Iron 14%. Diet Exchanges: 1 Starch, 2 Vegetable, 2 1/2 Medium-Fat Meat, 1 Fat. Carbohydrate Choices: 1 1/2

Scarecrow Cake

PREP: 10 MINUTES • BAKE: 55 MINUTES • COOL: 2 HOURS 10 MINUTES • 24 SERVINGS

3 cups all-purpose flour

2 1/2 cups sugar

1 cup baking cocoa

1 cup butter or margarine, softened

1 cup buttermilk

3/4 cup water

2 teaspoons baking soda

1 teaspoon vanilla

1/2 teaspoon salt

3 eggs

1 tub (16 ounces) vanilla ready-to-spread frosting

1 tablespoon chocolate-flavored syrup

1 package (4 ounces) waffle ice-cream bowls (10 bowls)

1 package (4.5 ounces) chewy fruit snack in 3-foot rolls (6 rolls)

holiday
DO-AHEAD *tip*

Bake the cake the night before, then have fun decorating the cake on Halloween afternoon.

1. Heat oven to 350°. Grease 12-cup bundt cake pan with shortening; lightly flour. Beat all ingredients except frosting, syrup, waffle bowls and fruit snack in large bowl with electric mixer on low speed 30 seconds, scraping bowl constantly. Beat on high speed 3 minutes, scraping bowl occasionally. Pour into pan.

2. Bake 50 to 55 minutes or until toothpick inserted in the center comes out clean. Cool 10 minutes; remove from pan to wire rack. Cool completely, about 2 hours.

3. Place cake on serving plate. Stir together frosting and syrup; reserve 1/4 cup of the frosting. Spread remaining frosting over cake. For straw hat, place 1 waffle bowl upside down in center of cake. Stack 5 more bowls on first bowl.

4. For hair, cut fruit snack into fourteen 6-inch strips and fourteen 5-inch strips. Cut each strip lengthwise to within 1 inch of top of strip. Place one 6-inch strip and 5-inch strip together, pressing together at uncut ends. Repeat with remaining strips. Randomly press pairs of strips on top two-thirds of cake, overlapping as needed and allowing strips to hang over side of cake. Spread reserved 1/4 cup frosting over top of hair.

5. For brim of hat, break remaining waffle bowls into 5 or 6 pieces each. Randomly press waffle pieces on top of cake, overlapping and tucking pieces as needed. Allow waffle pieces to hang over side of cake and over fruit snack strips. Cut pieces of remaining fruit snack for eyes and nose; press on cake.

one serving: Calories 345 (Calories from Fat 110; Fat 12g; (Saturated 8g); Cholesterol 50mg; Sodium 240mg; Carbohydrate 57g (Dietary Fiber 2g); Protein 4g. % Daily Value: Vitamin A 6%; Vitamin C 2%; Calcium 2%; Iron 8%. Diet Exchanges: 1 Starch, 3 Other Carbohydrates, 2 Fat. Carbohydrate Choices: 4

TREATS AND NO TRICKS PARTY

SERVES 8

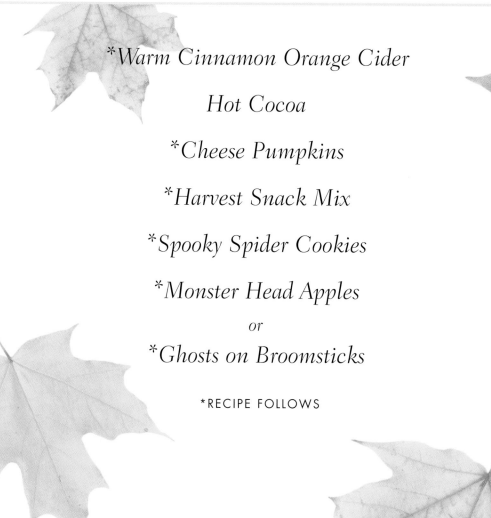

*Warm Cinnamon Orange Cider

Hot Cocoa

*Cheese Pumpkins

*Harvest Snack Mix

*Spooky Spider Cookies

*Monster Head Apples
or
*Ghosts on Broomsticks

*RECIPE FOLLOWS

Spooky Doorknob
Decorations

With these clever decorations it's not "What's behind that door?" it's what's on the door! Liven up any room with friendly spooks—they also look scary on your front door.

HOW TO DO IT:

1. Draw Halloween shapes (pumpkins, bats, ghosts, spiders) on felt squares using white pencil. Draw X, 1 1/2 × 1 1/2 inches, in center of each square, using pencil. (For spider and pumpkin cut squiggly line instead of X.)

2. Cut out shapes. Cut X along lines.

3. Decorate with puff paints; let dry. Pull over doorknob.

WHAT YOU NEED:

5- to 7-inch squares black, orange or white felt

White-lead pencil or chalk

Assorted puff paints

Paintbrushes

Warm Cinnamon Orange Cider

PREP: 5 MINUTES • COOK: 5 MINUTES • 8 SERVINGS (3/4 CUP EACH)

4 cups apple cider

2 cups orange juice

2 tablespoons red cinnamon candies

1 1/2 teaspoons whole allspice

1 tablespoon plus 1 1/2 teaspoons honey

holiday
shortcut

Pull out the slow cooker to make the party no fuss. Just pour the heated cider into a slow cooker, set on low and let everyone help themselves.

1. Heat all ingredients except honey to boiling; reduce heat. Cover and simmer 5 minutes.

2. Remove allspice. Stir in honey. Serve warm.

one serving: Calories 110 (Calories from Fat 0); Fat 0g; (Saturated 0g); Cholesterol 0mg; Sodium 5mg; Carbohydrate 27g (Dietary Fiber 0g); Protein 0g. % Daily Value: Vitamin A 2%; Vitamin C 18%; Calcium 0%; Iron 4%. Diet Exchanges: 2 Fruit. Carbohydrate Choices: 2

Cheese Pumpkins

PREP: 15 MINUTES • CHILL: 15 MINUTES • 8 PUMPKINS

8 tablespoons smoked Cheddar cold pack cheese food (from 8-ounce container), well chilled

2 teaspoons finely chopped peanuts

4 butter-flavored pretzel spindles or sticks, broken in half

16 tiny pieces fresh parsley leaves

1. Line small serving plate with waxed paper. Roll each level tablespoon cold pack cheese food into a ball; place on waxed paper-lined serving plate. Refrigerate 10 to 15 minutes for easier handling.

2. With end of toothpick draw ridges around balls to resemble pumpkins. Dip bottoms of cheese balls in chopped peanuts.

3. Just before serving, insert pretzel halves into cheese balls for pumpkin stems. Decorate with parsley for leaves. Store in refrigerator.

one pumpkin: Calories 55 (Calories from Fat 35); Fat 4g; (Saturated 2g); Cholesterol 15mg; Sodium 240mg; Carbohydrate 2g (Dietary Fiber 0g); Protein 3g. % Daily Value: Vitamin A 4%; Vitamin C 0%; Calcium 8%; Iron 0%. Diet Exchanges: 1/2 High-Fat Meat. Carbohydrate Choice: 0

holiday shortcut

Turn the pumpkin making into a family affair! Have one person roll the cheese into balls and another shape the balls into pumpkins, while someone else can dip the pumpkins and insert the pretzel. It's easy to double the recipe—make as many as you'd like!

Harvest Snack Mix

PREP: 5 MINUTES • 8 SERVINGS (1/2 CUP)

2 cups cinnamon-apple sweetened whole grain oat cereal rings

1 cup candy corn

1 cup salted peanuts

holiday
shortcut

This yummy treat is made with just three ingredients! It's so easy, you can let little ghosts and goblins mix up a batch for you. Another treat? It will keep up to 1 week in a tightly covered container at room temperature.

In a medium bowl, combine all ingredients; mix well.

one serving: Calories 240 (Calories from Fat 80); Fat 9g (Saturated 1g); Cholesterol 0mg; Sodium 120mg; Carbohydrate 35g (Dietary Fiber 2g); Protein 5g. % Daily Value: Vitamin A 2%; Vitamin C 2%; Calcium 4%; Iron 10%. Diet Exchanges: 2 Starch, 2 Fat. Carbohydrate Choices: 2

Spooky Spider Cookies

PREP: 45 MINUTES • 20 COOKIES

Black string licorice

20 orange crème-filled chocolate sandwich cookies

1 teaspoon chocolate ready-to-spread frosting (from 16-oz container)

40 miniature candy-coated chocolate pieces

1. For each cookie, cut eight 1 1/2-inch pieces of licorice for legs. Insert 4 pieces into each side of each cookie.

2. With frosting, attach 2 miniature chocolate pieces to top of each cookie for eyes.

one cookie: Calories 85 (Calories from Fat 25); Fat 3g; (Saturated 1g); Cholesterol 0mg; Sodium 85mg; Carbohydrate 14g (Dietary Fiber 0g); Protein 1g. % Daily Value: Vitamin A 0%; Vitamin C 0%; Calcium 0%; Iron 2%. Diet Exchanges: 1 Other Carbohydrates, 1/2 Fat. Carbohydrate Choices: 1

holiday twist
FLAVOR

Can't find orange crème-filled cookies? Vanilla-filled cookies work just fine. And if you'd like, you can use black licorice twists instead of the string. Cut the twists into 1 1/2-inch lengths, then cut the lengths vertically into thin strips.

HALLOWEEN

Monster Head Apples

PREP: 40 MINUTES • 8 APPLES

8 forks or flat wooden sticks with round ends

8 small apples

1 tub Betty Crocker Rich and Creamy vanilla ready-to-spread frosting

1/4 teaspoon green food color

16 fruit-flavored, ring-shaped hard candies

16 tiny, tart fruit-flavored candies

8 candy corn

8 wax lips or monster teeth

4 chewy fruit snack rolls

holiday
FLAVOR *twist*

These are not your typical apples-on-a-stick! The smooth, melted frosting holds decorations in place, so it's easy to be creative.

1. Cut waxed paper into 8 (8 × 6-inch) pieces; place on work surface. Insert fork into stem end of each apple for handle.

2. Remove lid and foil from can of frosting. Place can in microwave; microwave on High for 20 to 30 seconds or until frosting can be stirred smooth. Stir in green food color until well blended.

3. Holding 1 apple over large bowl to catch drips, spoon melted frosting over apple to coat. Place coated apple on piece of waxed paper. Repeat with remaining apples and frosting.

4. Press candies and wax lips into frosting on each apple to create face. Cut each snack roll in half crosswise; cut fringe on one long side. Wrap fringed snack roll pieces around top of apples for hair. Or, decorate as desired.

one apple: Calories 375 (Calories from Fat 80); Fat 9g (Saturated 8g); Cholesterol 0mg; Sodium 25mg; Carbohydrate 72g (Dietary Fiber 3g); Protein 1g. % Daily Value: Vitamin A 2%; Vitamin C 20%; Calcium 0%; Iron 0%. Diet Exchanges: 2 Fruit, 2 1/2 Other Carbohydrates, 2 Fat. Carbohydrate Choices: 4 1/2

Ghosts on Broomsticks

PREP: 30 MINUTES • STAND TIME: 45 MINUTES • 14 CANDIES

1 (.75-oz) any flavor chewy fruit snack in 3-foot roll, unwrapped

14 pretzel sticks (2 to 3 inches long)

2/3 cup white vanilla chips, melted

Miniature semisweet chocolate chips (52 chips)

holiday
DO-AHEAD *tip*

Get a jump on Halloween fun by making these witches the day before your party. Be prepared: these treats will magically disappear as soon as you serve them!

1. Line large cookie sheet with waxed paper or parchment paper. Unroll fruit snack roll. With kitchen scissors, cut 3/4-inch-long fringe on one long side of snack roll. Cut fringed roll into 2-inch pieces.

2. To make each "broomstick," wrap piece of fringe around one end of pretzel; press to seal. Place "broomsticks" on waxed paper-lined cookie sheet.

3. Drop rounded 1/2 teaspoonfuls of melted white chocolate chips crosswise onto pretzels; shape to resemble "ghosts" seated on "broomsticks."

4. Press 3 miniature chocolate chips into each "ghost" for eyes and mouth. Let stand at room temperature for about 45 minutes or in freezer for about 5 minutes or until set. Peel candies from waxed paper.

one candy: Calories 75 (Calories from Fat 35); Total Fat 4g; Saturated Fat 3g; Cholesterol 5 mg; Sodium 25mg; Total Carbohydrate 9g; Dietary Fiber 0g; Sugars 9g; Protein 1g. % Daily Value: Vitamin A 0%; Vitamin C 2%; Calcium 2%; Iron 0%. Diet Exchanges: 1/2 Other Carbohydrates, 1 Fat. Carbohydrate Choice : 1/2

THANKSGIVING

THE FIRST THANKSGIVING WAS HELD in 1621 by the pilgrims, who wanted to throw a feast to celebrate a successful harvest and to give thanks that they were well stocked for winter. The holiday we celebrate today, not to mention the monumental meal that goes along with it, are due in part to the perseverance of Sarah Josepha Hale, editor of *Godey's Lady's Book*. Hale crusaded for more than forty years to make Thanksgiving a nationally recognized holiday. President Abraham Lincoln finally granted her wish in 1863, fixing the date as the last Thursday in November.

DO-AHEAD THANKSGIVING DINNER

SERVES 6

Wine Spritzers

Cheese and Crackers

*Potatoes Stuffed with Pesto and Sun-Dried Tomatoes

*Best Brined Turkey Breast

*Marinated Vegetables

*Frosty Coffee Almond Pie

*RECIPES FOLLOW

Potatoes Stuffed with Pesto and Sun-Dried Tomatoes

PREP: 20 MINUTES • BAKE: 1 HOUR 35 MINUTES • 6 SERVINGS

3 large baking potatoes (8 to 10 ounces each)

1/4 to 1/2 cup milk

1/2 cup pesto

1/3 cup julienne sun-dried tomatoes packed in oil and herbs, drained

1/4 cup sliced ripe olives, well drained

1/2 cup finely shredded Parmesan cheese

Chopped fresh basil or parsley, if desired

Additional shredded Parmesan cheese, if desired

1. Heat oven to 375°. Gently scrub potatoes, but do not peel. Pierce potatoes several times with fork. Bake 1 hour to 1 hour 15 minutes or until potatoes are tender when pierced in center with fork. Let stand until cool enough to handle.

2. Cut each potato lengthwise in half; scoop out inside, leaving a thin shell. Mash potatoes and milk in medium bowl with potato masher or electric mixer until no lumps remain (amount of milk needed will vary depending on type of potato used). Stir in pesto, tomatoes, olives and 1/2 cup cheese. Fill potato shells with mashed potato mixture. Place on ungreased cookie sheet.

3. Bake about 20 minutes or until hot. Sprinkle with basil and additional cheese.

one serving: Calories 235 (Calories from Fat 135); Fat 15g; (Saturated 4g); Cholesterol 10mg; Sodium 410mg; Carbohydrate 19g (Dietary Fiber 2g); Protein 8g. % Daily Value: Vitamin A 6%; Vitamin C 12%; Calcium 22%; Iron 6%. Diet Exchanges: 1 Starch, 1 Vegetable, 3 Fat. Carbohydrate Choices: 1

holiday
DO-AHEAD *tip*

Refrigerate filled potatoes tightly covered up to 48 hours. To reheat in oven, bake uncovered on ungreased cookie sheet at 375° about 30 minutes or until hot.

To reheat in microwave, arrange potatoes in circle on 10-inch microwavable plate. Cover loosely with plastic wrap and microwave on High 12 to 15 minutes, rotating plate one-half turn after 5 minutes, until hot.

Best Brined Turkey Breast

SOAK: 12 HOURS • PREP: 10 MINUTES • BAKE: 2 HOURS 30 MINUTES • 8–12 SERVINGS

9 cups hot water

3/4 cup salt

1/2 cup sugar

4- to 6-pound bone-in whole turkey breast, thawed if frozen

1 onion, cut into eighths

2 fresh rosemary sprigs

4 fresh thyme sprigs

3 dried bay leaves

Salt and pepper, if desired

6 tablespoons butter or margarine, melted

1/4 cup dry white wine or chicken broth

holiday
DO-AHEAD *tip*

All the marinating is done ahead of Turkey Day, so you get a big jump on cooking the centerpiece of Thanksgiving dinner—plus there is no thawing time to factor into your menu planning! Just pop this in the oven and get ready for compliments.

1. Mix water, salt and sugar in 6-quart container or stockpot; stir until sugar and salt are dissolved. Add turkey. Cover and refrigerate at least 12 hours but no longer than 24 hours.

2. Heat oven to 325°. Remove turkey from brine, rinse thoroughly under cool running water and pat dry.

3. Place turkey, breast side up, on rack in large shallow roasting pan. Fill cavity with onion, rosemary, thyme and bay leaves. Sprinkle salt and pepper over turkey. Insert meat thermometer so tip is in thickest part of turkey and does not touch bone.

4. Mix butter and wine. Soak 16-inch square of cheesecloth in butter mixture until completely saturated; cover turkey completely with cheesecloth. Bake 1 hour 30 minutes.

5. Remove cheesecloth. Remove onion and herbs from turkey, but leave in pan. Bake 30 to 60 minutes longer or until thermometer reads 170° and juice of turkey is no longer pink when center is cut.

one serving: Calories 345 (Calories from Fat 170); Fat 19g; (Saturated 8g); Cholesterol 135mg; Sodium 470mg; Carbohydrate 1g (Dietary Fiber 0g); Protein 43g. % Daily Value: Vitamin A 6%; Vitamin C 0%; Calcium 2%; Iron 8%. Diet Exchanges: 6 Lean Meat. Carbohydrate Choices: 0

Personalized
Place Cards

These place cards will make family and friends feel special—and they can be made whenever you have the time!

WHAT YOU NEED:

Heavy cardstock paper, 5 × 8 inches or desired size

Metallic or colored pens or markers

Glass ball ornaments, at least 3 inches in diameter

Hot glue gun

Decorative twigs and pepperberries

4 to 5 inches 1/4-inch-wide ribbon

HOW TO DO IT:

1. Fold paper crosswise in half. Write each guest's name on card using metallic pen.

2. Remove tops from ornaments. Attach each ornament to card using hot glue gun.

3. Place twigs and pepperberries into ornaments. Tie ribbon around tops of ornaments.

Marinated Vegetables

PREP: 10 MINUTES • MARINATE: 3 HOURS • 8 SERVINGS

2/3 cup Italian vinaigrette dressing

4 cups cooked broccoli or Brussels sprouts

2 cups cherry tomatoes, cut in half

3 cups mushroom halves or fourths (8 ounces)

Lettuce leaves, if desired

1. Pour dressing over broccoli and tomatoes in large glass or plastic bowl. Cover and refrigerate at least 3 hours but no longer than 24 hours.

2. Add mushrooms to vegetables; toss until well coated. Drain before serving. Serve vegetables on lettuce.

one serving: Calories 135 (Calories from Fat 80); Fat 9g; (Saturated 1g); Cholesterol 5mg; Sodium 200mg; Carbohydrate 9g (Dietary Fiber 3g); Protein 4g. % Daily Value: Vitamin A 32%; Vitamin C 68%; Calcium 6%; Iron 4%. Diet Exchanges: 2 Vegetable, 2 Fat. Carbohydrate Choices: 1/2

holiday FLAVOR *twist*

Serve these festive marinated vegetables on individual serving plates that you've lined with kale leaves or red leaf lettuce. Sprinkle with toasted pine nuts for extra pizzazz.

Frosty Coffee Almond Pie

PREP: 15 MINUTES • FREEZE: 3 HOURS 15 MINUTES • STAND: 10 MINUTES • 8 SERVINGS

18 crème-filled chocolate sandwich cookies, finely crushed

3 tablespoons butter or margarine, melted

1 quart coffee ice cream, slightly softened

1/2 cup sliced almonds, toasted

1 cup hot fudge sauce, warmed

holiday
FLAVOR *twist*

Have fun picking the ice cream flavor for this special treat. You can use chocolate, vanilla, strawberry or any flavor that you like.

1. Mix crushed cookies and butter until well blended. Press on bottom and up side of ungreased pie plate, 9 × 1 1/4 inches. Freeze about 15 minutes or until firm.

2. Carefully spread ice cream evenly in crust. Sprinkle with almonds. Freeze about 3 hours or until firm.

3. Remove pie from freezer about 10 minutes before serving. Serve with hot fudge sauce. Store covered in freezer.

one serving: Calories 470 (Calories from Fat 215); Fat 24g; (Saturated 10g); Cholesterol 35mg; Sodium 360mg; Carbohydrate 60g (Dietary Fiber 4g); Protein 7g. % Daily Value: Vitamin A 10%; Vitamin C 0%; Calcium 12%; Iron 12%. Diet Exchanges: 2 Starch, 2 Other Carbohydrates, 4 Fat. Carbohydrate Choices: 4

AN UPDATED CLASSIC THANKSGIVING

SERVES 6

*"Cran-tinis"

*Bloody Mary Shrimp Cocktail

*Glazed Roasted Turkey

*Foolproof Gravy

*Cranberry Stuffing

*Slow Cooker Sweet Potatoes

*Green Beans with Shiitake Mushrooms

*Chocolate Pecan Pie

*Praline Pumpkin Date Bread

*RECIPES FOLLOW

"Cran-tinis"

PREP: 5 MINUTES • 4 SERVINGS

1 cup cranberry juice cocktail

1/2 cup citrus vodka or plain vodka

1/4 cup Triple Sec or orange juice

1 teaspoon fresh lime juice

Fresh cranberries, if desired

Lime slices, if desired

1. Fill martini shaker or 3-cup covered container half full with ice. Add all ingredients except cranberries and lime slices; cover and shake.

2. Pour into martini or tall stemmed glasses, straining the ice. Garnish glasses with fresh cranberries and lime slices on picks.

one serving: Calories 100 (Calories from Fat 0); Fat 0g; (Saturated 0g); Cholesterol 0mg; Sodium 0mg; Carbohydrate 11g (Dietary Fiber 0g); Protein 0g. % Daily Value: Vitamin A 0%; Vitamin C 34%; Calcium 0%; Iron 0%. Diet Exchanges: 1 Fruit, 1 Fat. Carbohydrate Choices: 1

holiday FLAVOR *twist*

Cran-tinis are sweeter than regular martinis. True martini drinkers may want to cut the cranberry juice cocktail in half. For a slightly less potent drink, serve Cran-tinis on the rocks and add a splash of sparkling water. And for extra dash, place a strip of lime peel in the bottom of each glass.

Bloody Mary Shrimp Cocktail

PREP: 30 MINUTES • COOK: 8 MINUTES • MARINATE: 2 HOURS • ABOUT 60 APPETIZERS

1 1/2 pounds cooked peeled deveined medium shrimp (about 60), thawed if frozen

1/2 cup tomato juice

1/4 cup vodka, if desired

1/2 teaspoon red pepper sauce

1/2 teaspoon sugar

1/2 teaspoon celery salt

2 tablespoons chopped fresh parsley

1 cup cocktail sauce

1/4 cup finely chopped green olives

holiday tip
DO-AHEAD

Don't marinate the shrimp more than 3 hours; staying longer in the tomato juice will toughen the shrimp.

holiday twist
FLAVOR

Place shrimp in an oversized martini glass (about 12 to 14 inches in diameter). Pour cocktail sauce mixture over shrimp, and garnish like a Bloody Mary with a skewer of colossal olives, a large lime wedge and a celery stick.

1. Arrange shrimp in single layer in rectangular glass or plastic dish, $11 \times 7 \times 1 \ 1/2$ inches.

2. Heat tomato juice, vodka and pepper sauce to boiling in 1-quart saucepan over medium-high heat. Stir in sugar; reduce heat. Simmer uncovered 5 minutes, stirring occasionally. Stir in celery salt and parsley; pour over shrimp. Cover and refrigerate 2 to 3 hours.

3. Mix cocktail sauce and olives; pour into small serving bowl. Remove shrimp from marinade with slotted spoon; arrange on serving platter. Serve shrimp with sauce and toothpicks.

one appetizer: Calories 10 (Calories from Fat 0); Fat 0g; (Saturated 0g); Cholesterol 20mg; Sodium 100mg; Carbohydrate 1g (Dietary Fiber 0g); Protein 2g. % Daily Value: Vitamin A 2%; Vitamin C 2%; Calcium 0%; Iron 0%. Diet Exchanges: one serving is Free. Carbohydrate Choices: 0

Turkey Basics

The favorite part of any holiday feast deserves to be treated right! No matter how you decide to serve up this noble bird, here are some great tips and techniques to help you prepare the perfect turkey.

Turkey Tips

1. Generally, the younger the turkey, the more tender the meat will be. Turkeys available today will usually be labeled "young," meaning 4 to 6 months old. The label may also indicate the sex (hen or tom).

2. When figuring quantities for whole turkeys, allow about 1 pound per person. The amount of sliced cooked turkey is about 50 percent of the weight of a whole turkey.

3. Be sure you start with a fully thawed turkey. Cooking charts and doneness times are based on a thawed turkey, and times and doneness can vary greatly if the turkey is not completely thawed.

4. For the moistest bird possible, don't overcook it. Use a meat thermometer to test for doneness. The internal temperature should reach 180° for whole birds and 170° for whole turkey breasts and bone-in or boneless pieces.

5. Turkey Help: If you have unanswered questions, you can call the USDA Meat and Poultry Hotline (800-535-4555), Butterball Turkey Talk Line (800-323-4848) or Reynolds Kitchens Turkey Tips Line (800-745-4000). And for more great ideas, visit BettyCrocker.com.

Thawing

QUICK THAW: Cover frozen turkey (in original packaging) with cold water, changing the water frequently. Allow about 30 minutes per pound for whole turkeys.

GRADUAL THAW: Refrigerate frozen turkey (in original packaging) on a tray to collect liquids. Allow about 24 hours per 5 pounds of whole turkey.

After thawing, remove the neck and giblets from the neck and body cavities. Rinse turkey inside and out with cold water, and drain. A thawed turkey may be refrigerated up to 2 days.

APPROXIMATE WEIGHT OF WHOLE TURKEY	THAWING TIME IN REFRIGERATOR
8 to 12 pounds	1 to 2 days
12 to 16 pounds	2 to 3 days
16 to 20 pounds	3 to 4 days
20 to 24 pounds	4 to 5 days

Stuffing

Prepare any stuffing just before stuffing the turkey. Pack the stuffing loosely into the neck cavity. Then, fasten neck skin to the back with skewers, and fold wings across the back with the tips touching. Next, loosely fill the body cavity. Tuck the drumsticks under the band of skin at the tail (or tie or skewer to the tail). When done, the center of the stuffing should reach 165°.

Roasting

1. Place turkey, breast side up, on a rack in a shallow roasting pan. Brush with melted butter, margarine or oil. If using an ovenproof thermometer, place it so the tip is in the thickest part of the inside thigh muscle and does not touch bone.

2. When two-thirds through the cooking time, cut band of skin at the tail or remove skewer holding drumsticks.

3. Check turkey for doneness with a meat thermometer. The temperature should be 180° and the juice should no longer be pink when you cut the center of a thigh.

4. If the turkey has turned golden brown but is not done, place a foil tent over the turkey if desired and continue roasting.

5. Let turkey stand for 15 to 20 minutes before carving.

Timetable for Roasting Turkey

Read-to-Cook Weight (pounds) WHOLE TURKEY	Approximate Roasting Time at 325° (hours)* STUFFED	NOT STUFFED
8 to 12	3 to 3 1/2	2 3/4 to 3
12 to 14	3 1/2 to 4	3 to 3 3/4
14 to 18	4 to 4 1/4	3 3/4 to 4 1/4
18 to 20	4 1/4 to 4 3/4	4 1/4 to 4 1/2
20 to 24	4 3/4 to 5 1/4	4 1/2 to 5

Begin checking turkey doneness about one hour before end of recommended roasting time. For prestuffed turkeys, follow package directions very carefully—do not use this timetable.

Glazed Roasted Turkey

PREP: 25 MINUTES • COOK: 10 MINUTES • ROAST: 4 HOURS • 18 SERVINGS

Cranberry Stuffing (page 171)

12-pound turkey, thawed if frozen

2 tablespoons butter or margarine, melted

Cranberry-Apple Glaze (at right)

holiday
DO-AHEAD *tip*

Be sure to plan ahead to thaw your turkey in time for Thanksgiving dinner. Check out the thawing guidelines on pages 166–167.

holiday
FLAVOR *twist*

The Cranberry-Apple Glaze is divine drizzled over vanilla ice cream. Make a batch to keep in the refrigerator for a quick last-minute holiday dessert. If you like, heat in the microwave.

1. Heat oven to 325°. Make Cranberry Stuffing. Stuff turkey just before roasting—not ahead of time. Fill wishbone area with stuffing first. Fasten neck skin to back with skewer. Fold wings across back with tips touching. Fill body cavity lightly. (Do not pack—stuffing will expand while cooking.) Tuck drumsticks under band of skin at tail, or tie together with heavy string, then tie to tail.

2. Place turkey, breast side up, on rack in shallow roasting pan. Brush with butter. Insert meat thermometer so tip is in thickest part of inside thigh muscle and does not touch bone. Do not add water.

3. Roast uncovered 3 hours 30 minutes to 4 hours. Thermometer will read 180° when turkey is done, and drumstick should move easily when lifted or twisted. Roast until juice is no longer pink when center of thigh is cut. Thermometer placed in center of stuffing will read 165° when done. If a meat thermometer is not used, begin testing for doneness after about 3 hours.

4. Make Cranberry-Apple Glaze while turkey is roasting. Brush glaze on turkey about 20 minutes before turkey is done.

5. Place a tent of aluminum foil loosely over turkey when it begins to turn golden. When two-thirds done, cut band of skin or string holding legs. When turkey is done, place on warm platter and cover with aluminum foil to keep warm. Let stand about 15 minutes for easiest carving.

6. To serve, brush again with glaze before carving. Cover and refrigerate any remaining turkey and stuffing separately.

Cranberry-Apple Glaze

1 can (8 ounces) jellied cranberry sauce

1/4 cup apple jelly

1/4 cup light corn syrup

Mix all ingredients in 1-quart saucepan. Cook over medium heat about 5 minutes, stirring occasionally, until melted and smooth

one serving: 540 Calories (Calories from Fat 255); Fat 28g; (Saturated 12g); Cholesterol 170mg; Sodium 510mg; Carbohydrate 22g (Dietary Fiber 1g); Protein 50g. % Daily Value: Vitamin A 10%; Vitamin C 0%; Calcium 6%; Iron 16%. Diet Exchanges: 1 Starch, 1/2 Fruit, 6 1/2 Lean Meat, 1 Vegetable, 1 1/2 Fat. Carbohydrate Choices: 1 1/2

Foolproof Gravy

PREP: 5 MINUTES • COOK: 5 MINUTES • 2 CUPS

1/4 cup turkey drippings (fat and juices from roasted turkey)

1/4 cup all-purpose flour

2 cups liquid (juices from roasted turkey, broth, water)

Browning sauce, if desired

1/2 teaspoon salt

1/2 teaspoon pepper

holiday
FLAVOR *twist*

For added flavor, use vegetable cooking water, tomato juice, vegetable juice or wine as part of the liquid.

1. Pour drippings from turkey roasting pan into bowl, leaving brown particles in pan. Return 1/4 cup drippings to roasting pan. (Measure accurately because too little fat makes gravy lumpy.) Beat in flour with wire whisk. (Measure accurately so gravy is not greasy.)

2. Cook over medium heat, stirring constantly, until mixture is smooth and bubbly; remove from heat. Stir in liquid. Heat to boiling, stirring constantly. Boil and stir 1 minute. Stir in a few drops of browning sauce. Stir in salt and pepper.

one-quarter cup: Calories 55 (Calories from Fat 35); Fat 4g; (Saturated 1g); Cholesterol 5mg; Sodium 400mg; Carbohydrate 3g (Dietary Fiber 0g); Protein 2g. % Daily Value: Vitamin A 0%; Vitamin C 0%; Calcium 0%; Iron 2%. Diet Exchanges: 1 Fat. Carbohydrate Choices: 0

Cranberry Stuffing

PREP: 20 MINUTES • COOK: 5 MINUTES • 18 SERVINGS (1/2 CUP EACH)

1 cup butter or margarine

3 medium celery stalks (with leaves), chopped (1 1/2 cups)

3/4 cup finely chopped onion

9 cups soft bread cubes (15 slices)

1/2 cup dried cranberries or golden raisins

2 tablespoons chopped fresh or 1 1/2 teaspoons dried sage leaves

1 tablespoon chopped fresh or 1 teaspoon dried thyme leaves

1 1/2 teaspoons salt

1/2 teaspoon pepper

1. Melt butter in 10-inch skillet over medium heat. Cook celery and onion in butter, stirring frequently, until onion is tender. Stir in about one-third of the bread cubes. Place in large bowl. Add remaining bread cubes and ingredients; toss.

2. Stuff turkey just before roasting.

one serving: 160 Calories (Calories from Fat 100); Fat 11g; (Saturated 7g); Cholesterol 30mg; Sodium 380mg; Carbohydrate 14g (Dietary Fiber 1g); Protein 2g. % Daily Value: Vitamin A 8%; Vitamin C 0%; Calcium 2%; Iron 4%. Diet Exchanges: 1 Starch, 2 Fat. Carbohydrate Choices: 1

holiday **FLAVOR** *twist*

You can vary the flavor of the stuffing by using other dried fruit in place of the dried cranberries. Try golden raisins, chopped prunes, dried cherries or dried blueberries.

Slow Cooker Sweet Potatoes

PREP: 15 MINUTES • COOK: 8 HOURS • 6 SERVINGS

6 medium sweet potatoes or yams (2 pounds), peeled and cut into 1-inch cubes

1 1/2 cups applesauce

2/3 cup packed brown sugar

3 tablespoons butter or margarine, melted

1 teaspoon ground cinnamon

1/2 cup chopped nuts, toasted

holiday FLAVOR *twist*

Many varieties of sweet potatoes are available. Although the variety of sweet potatoes with dark orange skin is often labeled as "yams," true yams are not available in our supermarkets. The very light-colored sweet potatoes are not as sweet and are drier than the darker-skinned ones. We like the darker sweet potatoes (or "yams") for this dish.

1. Place sweet potatoes in 2- to 3 1/2-quart slow cooker. Mix remaining ingredients except nuts; spoon over potatoes.

2. Cover and cook on low heat setting 6 to 8 hours or until potatoes are very tender.

3. Meanwhile, cook nuts in ungreased heavy skillet over medium-low heat 5 to 7 minutes, stirring frequently until browning begins, then stirring constantly until golden brown and fragrant; set aside. Sprinkle nuts over sweet potatoes.

one serving: Calories 345 (Calories from Fat 120); Fat 13g; (Saturated 4g); Cholesterol 15mg; Sodium 60mg; Carbohydrate 58g (Dietary Fiber 5g); Protein 3g. % Daily Value: Vitamin A 100%; Vitamin C 24%; Calcium 6%; Iron 6%. Diet Exchanges: 1 Starch, 3 Other Carbohydrates, 2 Fat. Carbohydrate Choices: 4

Edible Centerpiece

For true Thanksgiving bounty, it's hard to beat a centerpiece that you and your guests can actually eat! This is also a great way to serve appetizers before dinner.

HOW TO DO IT:

1. Place tile on table or counter. Arrange fruit on tile.

2. Select firm fruits, such as apples, pears or oranges, to be candleholders. Make sure fruit stands upright on the table and won't tip over; cut a thin slice off bottom if necessary. Cut a hole through stem end of the fruit with apple corer; slide candle into hole.

3. Fill dishes with chocolates and nuts. Arrange crackers and cheese on tile with spreader to serve.

WHAT YOU NEED:

12-inch glazed or ceramic square tile (from home supply store)

Fresh fruits, such as apples, pears, oranges and grapes

Apple corer

Tapered candles, about 1 inch in diameter at base

2 small dishes

Assorted chocolates, nuts and crackers

Large wedge of cheese

Cheese spreader or knife

Green Beans with Shiitake Mushrooms

PREP: 15 MINUTES • COOK: 16 MINUTES • 6 SERVINGS

1 1/2 pounds fresh green beans

1/4 cup slivered almonds

6 ounces fresh shiitake mushrooms

1 tablespoon olive or vegetable oil

1 tablespoon sesame oil

3 cloves garlic, finely chopped

2 tablespoons soy sauce

holiday shortcut

If you're pressed for time, you can purchase two 12-ounce bags of washed fresh green beans. You'll find them in the produce section of your supermarket.

1. Leave beans whole, or cut into 1-inch pieces. Place steamer basket in 1/2 inch water in saucepan or skillet (water should not touch bottom of basket). Place green beans in steamer basket. Cover tightly and heat to boiling; reduce heat. Steam 10 minutes.

2. Meanwhile, cook almonds in ungreased heavy skillet over medium-low heat 5 to 7 minutes, stirring frequently until browning begins, then stirring constantly until golden brown and fragrant.

3. Remove tough stems of mushrooms; cut mushrooms into 1/4-inch slices. Heat olive and sesame oils in 12-inch skillet over medium heat. Cook mushrooms and garlic in oil 3 minutes, stirring occasionally. Stir in soy sauce and green beans. Cook 2 to 3 minutes or until mushrooms are tender. Sprinkle with almonds.

one serving: Calories 100 (Calories from Fat 65); Fat 7g; (Saturated 1g); Cholesterol 0mg; Sodium 310mg; Carbohydrate 9g (Dietary Fiber 4g); Protein43g. % Daily Value: Vitamin A 12%; Vitamin C 4%; Calcium 6%; Iron 8%. Diet Exchanges: 2 Vegetables, 1 Fat. Carbohydrate Choices: 1/2

Chocolate Pecan Pie

PREP: 20 MINUTES • BAKE: 50 MINUTES • COOL: 30 MINUTES • CHILL: 2 HOURS • 8 SERVINGS

Best Flaky Pastry (below)

2/3 cup sugar

1/3 cup butter or margarine, melted

1 cup corn syrup

1/2 teaspoon salt

3 eggs

1 cup pecan halves or broken pecans

1 package (6 ounces) semisweet chocolate chips (1 cup)

holiday FLAVOR *twist*

Make this luscious pie even more festive by garnishing with whipped cream and chocolate leaves that you can buy at the store.

1. Heat oven to 375°. Make Best Flaky Pastry.

2. Beat sugar, butter, corn syrup, salt and eggs in large bowl with hand beater. Stir in pecans and chocolate chips. Pour into pastry-line pie plate. Cover edge with 2- to 3-inch strip of aluminum foil to prevent excessive browning; remove foil during last 15 minutes of baking.

3. Bake 40 to 50 minutes or until set. Cool 30 minutes. Refrigerate about 2 hours until chilled.

Best Flaky Pastry

1 cup all-purpose flour

1/4 teaspoon salt

1/3 cup plus 1 tablespoon shortening

2 to 3 tablespoons cold water

1. Mix flour and salt in medium bowl. Cut in shortening, using pastry blender or crisscrossing 2 knives, until particles are size of small peas. Sprinkle with cold water, 1 tablespoon at a time, tossing with fork until all flour is moistened and pastry almost leaves side of bowl (1 to 2 teaspoons more water can be added if necessary).

2. Gather pastry into a ball. Shape into flattened round on lightly floured surface. Roll pastry, using floured rolling pin, into circle 2 inches larger than upside-down pie plate, 9 × 1 1/4 inches. Place in pie plate; flute as desired.

one serving: Calories 625 (Calories from Fat 315); Fat 35g; (Saturated 13g); Cholesterol 100mg; Sodium 350mg; Carbohydrate 75g (Dietary Fiber 3g); Protein 6g. % Daily Value: Vitamin A 8%; Vitamin C 0%; Calcium 2%; Iron 10%. Diet Exchanges: 2 Starch, 3 Other Carbohydrates, 6 1/2 Fat. Carbohydrate Choices: 5

Praline Pumpkin Date Bread

PREP: 15 MINUTES • BAKE: 1 HOUR • COOL: 1 HOUR 10 MINUTES •
2 LOAVES (24 SLICES EACH)

Praline Topping (below)

1 2/3 cups sugar

2/3 cup vegetable oil

2 teaspoons vanilla

4 eggs

1 can (15 ounces) pumpkin (not pumpkin pie mix)

3 cups all-purpose flour

2 teaspoons baking soda

1 teaspoon ground cinnamon

3/4 teaspoon salt

1/2 teaspoon baking powder

1/2 teaspoon ground cloves

1 cup chopped dates

holiday *tip*
DO-AHEAD

Want a jump-start on the festivities? Bake this yummy bread when you have time. Then wrap the baked bread tightly. You can store the bread at room temperature for up to 4 days or refrigerate up to 10 days. Just watch out for nibblers!

1. Move oven rack to low position so that tops of pans will be in center of oven. Heat oven to 350°. Grease bottoms only of 2 loaf pans, 8 1/2 × 4 1/2 × 2 1/2 inches, or 1 loaf pan, 9 × 5 × 3 inches, with shortening. Make Praline Topping; set aside.

2. Mix sugar, oil, vanilla, eggs and pumpkin in large bowl. Stir in remaining ingredients except dates until well blended. Stir in dates. Pour batter into pans. Sprinkle with topping.

3. Bake 8-inch loaves 50 to 60 minutes, 9-inch loaf 1 hour 10 minutes to 1 hour 20 minutes, or until toothpick inserted in center comes out clean. Cool 10 minutes. Loosen sides of loaves from pans; remove from pans to wire rack. Cool completely, about 1 hour, before slicing.

Praline Topping

1/3 cup packed brown sugar

1/3 cup chopped pecans

1 tablespoon butter or margarine, softened

Mix all ingredients until crumbly.

one slice: Calories 110 (Calories from Fat 35); Fat 4g; (Saturated 1g); Cholesterol 20mg; Sodium 100mg; Carbohydrate 18g (Dietary Fiber 1g); Protein 2g. % Daily Value: Vitamin A 28%; Vitamin C 0%; Calcium 0%; Iron 4%. Diet Exchanges: 1 Starch, 1/2 Fat. Carbohydrate Choices: 1

HANUKKAH

HANUKKAH, ALSO CALLED THE FESTIVAL OF LIGHTS, celebrates a miracle that took place more than two thousand years ago. The Syrian-Greeks had invaded Jerusalem and taken over the holy temple. A small army of Jews, led by Judah Maccabee, managed to defeat the invaders and regain control of the temple. To rededicate the temple and celebrate their victory, the Jews relit the temple's light, but there was only enough oil for one day. Here's where the miracle comes in: Instead of burning out after one day, the light remained lit for eight entire days! Today, candles on a menorah symbolize those eight nights of light.

HANUKKAH DINNER

SERVES 6

*Honeyed Carrots

*Salmon with Mint Sauce

or

*Braised Brisket of Beef

*Latkes

*Ginger Applesauce

*Hanukkah Honey Cookies

*Easy Doughnuts

*RECIPE FOLLOWS

Honeyed Carrots

PREP: 20 MINUTES • COOK: 15 MINUTES • 6 SERVINGS

6 medium carrots, cut into julienne strips (3/4 pound)

6 medium green onions, sliced (1/3 cup)

1/3 cup honey

1 tablespoon vegetable oil

1 tablespoon lemon juice

1/2 teaspoon salt

1. Heat 1 inch water (salted if desired) to boiling in 10-inch skillet. Add carrots. Heat to boiling; reduce heat. Cover and simmer about 5 minutes or until tender; drain. Remove from skillet; set aside.

2. Cook remaining ingredients in same skillet over low heat, stirring frequently, until bubbly. Stir in carrots. Cook uncovered 2 to 3 minutes, stirring occasionally, until carrots are glazed.

one serving: Calories 105 (Calories from Fat 20); Fat 2g; (Saturated 0g); Cholesterol 0mg; Sodium 220mg; Carbohydrate 24g (Dietary Fiber 3g); Protein 2g. % Daily Value: Vitamin A 100%; Vitamin C 6%; Calcium 2%; Iron 2%. Diet Exchanges: 1 Other Carbohydrates, 2 Vegetable. Carbohydrate Choices: 1 1/2

holiday history

Why honeyed carrots? Honey is a traditional Hanukkah treat for Sephardic Jews who come from Greece and Turkey.

Salmon with Mint Sauce

PREP: 15 MINUTES • CHILL: 1 HOUR • BROIL: 6 MINUTES • 6 SERVINGS

Mint Sauce (below)

1 1/2 pounds salmon or other medium-firm fish fillets, cut into 6 serving pieces

1 teaspoon grated lemon peel

1/2 teaspoon salt

1/4 teaspoon pepper

holiday tip
DO-AHEAD

You can prepare the Mint Sauce up to 2 days before to make cooking this dinner even easier.

1. Prepare Mint Sauce.

2. If fish fillets are large, cut into 6 servings pieces. Sprinkle fish with lemon peel, salt and pepper.

3. Set oven control to broil. Spray broiler pan rack with cooking spray. Place fish on rack in broiler pan. Broil with tops about 4 inches from heat 5 to 6 minutes or until fish flakes easily with fork. Serve with sauce.

Mint Sauce

3/4 cup plain nonfat yogurt

1 tablespoon chopped fresh or 1 teaspoon dried mint leaves

1 tablespoon mayonnaise or salad dressing

1 teaspoon grated orange peel

1 clove garlic, finely chopped

Mix all ingredients. Cover and refrigerate at least 1 hour.

one serving: Calories 185 (Calories from Fat 80); Fat 9g (Saturated 1g); Cholesterol 65mg; Sodium 280mg; Carbohydrate 2g (Dietary Fiber 0g); Protein 24g. % Daily Value: Vitamin A 2%; Vitamin C 0%; Calcium 8%; Iron 4%. Diet Exchanges: 3 1/2 Lean Meat. Carbohydrate Choices: 0

Braised Brisket of Beef

PREP: 20 MINUTES • BAKE: 3 HOURS • STAND: 10 MINUTES • 12 SERVINGS

3-pound beef brisket (not corned-style)

1 1/2 cups white wine vinegar

1/4 cup firmly packed brown sugar

1 teaspoon dried basil leaves

1/2 teaspoon salt

1 bottle (12 ounces) chili sauce

2 medium onions, thinly sliced

holiday
DO-AHEAD *tip*

Marinating the brisket the night before saves time in the morning—and the unattended cooking leaves you more time for the rest of the dinner and visiting with your quests.

1. Place brisket in resealable food storage plastic bag or 3-quart casserole, cutting meat in half if necessary to fit. In medium bowl, combine vinegar, brown sugar, basil, salt and chili sauce; blend well. Pour over brisket; turn to coat. Seal bag or cover dish. Refrigerate at least 8 hours or up to 24 hours, turning once.

2. Heat oven to 325°. Place beef and marinade in Dutch oven or 3-quart casserole. Place onions over top; cover. Bake at 325° for 2 hours, basting twice with marinade.

3. Remove cover; bake an additional 1 hour or until beef is tender, basting frequently. Remove from oven, cover and let stand 10 minutes.

4. To serve, thinly slice across grain of beef; arrange on serving platter. With slotted spoon, place onions over beef. Discard cooking liquid.

one serving: Calories 170 (Calories from Fat 70); Fat 8g (Saturated 3g); Cholesterol 65mg; Sodium 350mg; Carbohydrate 11g (Dietary Fiber 1g); Protein 25g. % Daily Value: Vitamin A 6%; Vitamin C 2%; Calcium 2%; Iron 14%. Diet Exchanges: 1 Vegetable, 1/2 Other Carbohydrates, 2 Lean Meat. Carbohydrate Choices: 1

Latkes

PREP: 15 MINUTES • COOK: 20 MINUTES • 16 PANCAKES

4 medium baking potatoes (1 1/2 pounds), peeled

4 large eggs, beaten

1 small onion, finely chopped (1/4 cup)

1/4 cup all-purpose flour

2 tablespoons finely chopped fresh parsley

1/2 teaspoon salt

1/4 teaspoon pepper

About 1/4 cup vegetable oil

1. Shred enough potatoes to measure 4 cups. Rinse well; drain and pat dry.

2. Mix potatoes, eggs, onion, flour, parsley, salt and pepper. Heat 2 tablespoons of the oil in 12-inch skillet over medium heat. For each pancake, pour about 1/4 cup batter into skillet. Flatten each with spatula into pancake about 4 inches in diameter.

3. Cook pancakes about 2 minutes on each side or until golden brown. Cover to keep warm while cooking remaining pancakes. Repeat with remaining batter; as batter stands, liquid and potatoes will separate, so stir to mix as necessary. Add oil as needed to prevent sticking.

one pancake: Calories 70 (Calories from Fat 35); Fat 4g (Saturated 1g); Cholesterol 55mg; Sodium 90mg; Carbohydrate 7g (Dietary Fiber 1g); Protein 2g. % Daily Value: Vitamin A 2%; Vitamin C 2%; Calcium 0%; Iron 2%. Diet Exchanges: 1/2 Starch, 1/2 Fat. Carbohydrate Choices: 1/2

holiday history

Legend has it that latkes were served by the wives of the Maccabees to their husbands as they prepared to drive the ancient Syrians from their land. Latkes are eaten during Hanukkah to commemorate the victory.

Ginger Applesauce

4 medium cooking apples, peeled and each cut into fourths

1/2 cup water

1/4 cup packed brown sugar

2 tablespoons finely chopped crystallized ginger

1/4 teaspoon ground cinnamon

1/8 teaspoon ground ginger

holiday
FLAVOR *twist*

The ginger and cinnamon add a lovely flavor to this applesauce, but if your children like their applesauce plain, just leave out the spices.

1. Heat apples and water to boiling in 3-quart saucepan over medium heat, stirring occasionally; reduce heat. Cover and simmer 5 to 10 minutes, stirring occasionally to break up apples, until apples are tender.

2. Stir in remaining ingredients. Heat to boiling. Boil and stir 1 minute. Cover and refrigerate 3 hours or until chilled but no longer than 3 days.

one serving: Calories 95 (Calories from Fat 0); Fat 0g; (Saturated 0g); Cholesterol 0mg; Sodium1 5mg; Carbohydrate 24g (Dietary Fiber 2g); Protein 0g. % Daily Value: Vitamin A 0%; Vitamin C 2%; Calcium 0%; Iron 0%. Diet Exchanges: 1 1/2 Fruit . Carbohydrate Choices: 1 1/2

Relaxing Milk Bath

December is always hectic—wouldn't it be "miraculous" to find the time for pampering? This easy present will delight everyone who receives it, and it's so easy for little ones to join in the fun!

Just spoon this soothing mixture into pretty Hanukkah boxes or bags (see photo for ideas) and give to family and friends during the Hanukkah season. Include a small candle and they'll be able to enjoy a relaxing bath in candlelight at home, perhaps while nibbling a bit of Hanukkah gelt.

WHAT YOU NEED & HOW TO DO IT:

For each gift box mix together 1 cup salt, 1 cup baking soda and 1 cup nonfat dry milk. To use, add 1 cup bath mixture to warm bath water. Can be stored in airtight container up to 1 year.

Hanukkah Honey Cookies

PREP: 20 MINUTES • BAKE: 8 MINUTES PER SHEET • COOL: 30 MINUTES •
ABOUT 3 1/2 DOZEN COOKIES

1/3 cup powdered sugar	2 3/4 cups all-purpose flour
1/3 cup butter or margarine, softened	1 teaspoon baking soda
2/3 cup honey	1/2 teaspoon salt
1 teaspoon almond extract	Almond Glaze (below)
1 egg	Decorators' Frosting (below)

holiday
DO-AHEAD *tip*

Bake these delicious cookies the day before your Hannukah dinner, and let the kids spend the afternoon decorating them—instant fun!

1. Heat oven to 375°. Lightly grease cookie sheets.

2. Mix powdered sugar, butter, honey, almond extract and egg in large bowl. Stir in flour, baking soda and salt.

3. Roll dough 1/8 inch thick on lightly floured surface. Cut with 2-inch cookie cutters. Place about 1 inch apart on cookie sheet.

4. Bake 7 to 8 minutes or until light brown. Immediately remove from cookie sheet to wire rack; cool completely. Frost with Almond Glaze and decorate with Decorators' Frosting.

Almond Glaze

2 cups powdered sugar	2 to 3 tablespoons water
1/4 teaspoon almond extract	

Mix powdered sugar, almond extract and 2 tablespoons water until smooth. Stir in remaining 1 tablespoon water, 1 teaspoon at a time, until spreading consistency.

Decorators' Frosting

1 cup powdered sugar	3 or 4 drops blue food color
3 to 5 teaspoons water	

Mix powdered sugar and enough water to make a frosting that can be easily drizzled or used in a decorating bag yet hold its shape. Stir in food color.

one cookie: Calories 100 (Calories from Fat 20); Fat 2g (Saturated 1g); Cholesterol 10mg; Sodium 70mg; Carbohydrate 20g (Dietary Fiber 0g); Protein 1g. % Daily Value: Vitamin A 0%; Vitamin C 0%; Calcium 0%; Iron 2%. Diet Exchanges: 1/2 Starch, 1/2 Other Carbohydrate, 1/2 Fat. Carbohydrate Choices: 1

Easy Doughnuts

PREP: 10 MINUTES • FRY: 8 MINUTES • 10 DOUGHNUTS

Oil for frying

1 can (12 ounces) refrigerated fluffy buttermilk biscuits

Granulated or powdered sugar, if desired

holiday history

At Hannukah, people eat fried foods like donuts (*sufganiyot* in Hebrew) to celebrate the miracle that the remaining oil in the Temple—only enough to burn for one day—actually lasted for eight.

1. Heat oil (2 inches) in Dutch oven or deep fryer to 375°.

2. Separate dough into 10 biscuits. Cut hole in center of each biscuit using a small round cookie cutter.

3. Fry biscuits and holes in hot oil for 1 to 2 minutes on each side or until deep golden brown. Carefully remove from oil (do not prick surfaces). Drain on paper towels. Roll warm doughnuts and holes in sugar; serve warm.

one doughnut: Calories 135 (Calories from Fat 65); Fat 7g (Saturated 2g); Cholesterol 0mg; Sodium 410mg; Carbohydrate 16g (Dietary Fiber 1g); Protein 2g. % Daily Value: Vitamin A 0%; Vitamin C 0%; Calcium 0%; Iron 4%. Diet Exchanges: 1 Starch, 1 Fat. Carbohydrate Choices: 1

CHRISTMAS

CHRISTMAS IS A JOYOUS CHRISTIAN CELEBRATION that commemorates the birth of Christ. The holiday tends to be filled with so much generosity and goodwill that it often spills over to people of all religious backgrounds and beliefs. It's a busy time of year—people hurry from store to store looking for gifts, and weekends fill up quickly with holiday parties. Anticipation builds as presents stack up under the tree and, for children at least, the countdown to Christmas seems to take forever. The festive menus that follow offer some relief to time-crunched calendars and busy holiday hosts.

MERRY CHRISTMAS DINNER

SERVES 12

*Noel Spritzer

*Puff Pastry Wreath with Brie

*Sweet and Spicy Rubbed Ham

*Pear and Blue Cheese Salad

*Cheesy Scalloped Potatoes

*Pine Tree Parmesan Breadsticks

*Dark Chocolate Raspberry Fondue

Assorted Christmas Cookies

*RECIPES FOLLOW

Noel Spritzer

PREP: 5 MINUTES • 6 SERVINGS (3/4 CUP EACH)

2 cups chilled dry white wine, nonalcoholic wine or apple juice

1 cup chilled cran-apple juice cocktail

1 cup chilled sparkling water

Apple slices, if desired

Fresh mint, if desired

1. Mix wine, juice drink and sparkling water.

2. Serve over ice. Garnish with apple slices and mint.

one serving: Calories 95 (Calories from Fat 0); Fat 0g; (Saturated 0g); Cholesterol 0mg; Sodium 5mg; Carbohydrate 11g (Dietary Fiber 0g); Protein 0g. % Daily Value: Vitamin A 0%; Vitamin C 24%; Calcium 0%; Iron 2%. Diet Exchanges: 1 Fruit, 1/2 Fat. Carbohydrate Choices: 1

holiday
FLAVOR *twist*

Try your favorite juice flavors, or investigate a more unusual blend such as guava-pineapple, in this refreshing mixture of wine and sparkling water. This recipe can easily be doubled or tripled.

Puff Pastry Wreath with Brie

PREP: 20 MINUTES • CHILL: 10 MINUTES • BAKE: 28 MINUTES • 12–15 SERVINGS

1 sheet frozen puff pastry, thawed
(from 17.3-ounce package)

1 round (14 to 15 ounces) Brie cheese

1 egg

1 tablespoon milk

1 teaspoon chopped fresh rosemary leaves

Red currants or cranberries

Fresh bay leaves, if desired

holiday tip
DO-AHEAD

You can make this impressive puff pastry wreath up to 2 days before serving. After baking, place the wreath on the serving tray, cover tightly with plastic wrap and store at room temperature.

holiday hint

Want a more casual presentation? Use a bell- or star-shaped cookie cutter to cut pastry into 24 pieces, but do not make wreath; bake pastry cutouts as directed. Arrange puff pastry cutouts around cheese. Garnish with fresh thyme and fresh cranberries.

1. Heat oven to 400°. Place pastry on lightly floured surface. Cut pastry with 3-inch leaf-shaped cookie cutter dipped in flour to prevent sticking to make about 24 cutouts. Place cheese on ungreased cookie sheet; arrange pastry leaves in circle around cheese. Remove cheese. Cover and refrigerate pastry wreath 5 to 10 minutes.

2. Beat egg and milk with fork or wire whisk until well blended. Brush egg mixture on top of pastry wreath; sprinkle with chopped rosemary. Bake 15 to 18 minutes or until golden brown. Carefully remove pastry wreath from cookie sheet; place on serving platter.

3. Make impression in top of cheese about 1/4 inch deep with leaf cutter; remove cutter. Gently scrape and remove rind from leaf design, using spoon. Place cheese on ungreased cookie sheet.

4. Bake cheese 8 to 10 minutes or until cheese is soft and partially melted. Place cheese in center of pastry wreath. Garnish with currants and bay leaves.

one serving: Calories 210 (Calories from Fat 145); Fat 16g; (Saturated 8g); Cholesterol 70mg; Sodium 260mg; Carbohydrate 8g (Dietary Fiber 0g); Protein 9g. % Daily Value: Vitamin A 4%; Vitamin C 0%; Calcium 6%; Iron 6%. Diet Exchanges: 1/2 Starch, 1 High-Fat Meat, 2 1/2 Fat. Carbohydrate Choices: 1/2

Sweet and Spicy Rubbed Ham

PREP: 10 MINUTES • BAKE: 1 HOUR, 30 MINUTES • STAND: 15 MINUTES • 20 SERVINGS

6- to 8-pound fully cooked smoked bone-in ham

1/2 cup packed brown sugar

1/3 cup maple-flavored syrup

1/2 teaspoon ground mustard

1/8 teaspoon ground cinnamon

1/8 teaspoon ground ginger

1/8 teaspoon ground cloves

Dash of nutmeg

holiday FLAVOR twist

Although this ham is delicious on its own, you may want to offer some type of condiment or sauce. Honey mustard, Dijon mustard, chutney and fruit sauce are excellent accompaniments.

holiday hint

Want an impressive look, with very little effort? A simple garnish of red grapes, watercress and cinnamon sticks is easy and impressive.

1. Heat oven to 325°. Line shallow roasting pan with aluminum foil. Place ham, cut side down, on rack in pan. Insert ovenproof meat thermometer in thickest part of ham. Bake uncovered about 1 hour 30 minutes or until thermometer reads 135 to 140°.

2. While ham is baking, mix remaining ingredients. Brush over ham during last 30 minutes of baking.

3. Cover ham loosely with aluminum foil and let stand 10 to 15 minutes for easier carving.

one serving: Calories 130 (Calories from Fat 35); Fat 4g (Saturated 1g); Cholesterol 35 mg; Sodium 800mg; Carbohydrate 10g (Dietary Fiber 0g); Protein 14g. % Daily Value: Vitamin A 0%; Vitamin C 0%; Calcium 0%; Iron 6%. Diet Exchanges: 1/2 Other Carbohydrates, 2 Very Lean Meat, 1/2 Fat. Carbohydrate Choices: 1/2

Golden Glow Candy Wreath

Adapt this wreath to your holiday color scheme. If it's silver, use silver-wrapped candies and silver, green or red ribbons. If you prefer a red color scheme, scan the candy section for red-wrapped candies, and use red, gold, silver or green ribbons.

WHAT YOU NEED:

1 coat hanger

Wire cutters

Cloth tape (duct tape)

Embroidery floss or thin all-purpose string, about 3 1/2 yards

2 pounds butterscotch or gold-foil wrapped hard candies

String of small battery-powered lights

Red ribbon

HOW TO DO IT:

1. Snip coat hanger at base of hook, using wire cutters, leaving approximately 3 feet of wire. Shape wire into 8-inch circle, twisting ends of wire back around circle. Secure ends to circle with tape.

2. Tie a 6-inch piece of floss to wire circle. Place end of 3 candy wrappers on wire; tie knot in floss to secure candies to circle. Continue in this manner, arranging candy to the inside and outside of the circle.

3. Weave string of lights in wreath to create a glowing golden halo of candy. Decorate wreath with ribbon.

Sparkling Place Cards

You can easily change the color of the sugar to match your color scheme. This is fun for kids—especially coloring the sugar. See page 210 for how to color sugar.

HOW TO DO IT:

1. Carefully remove top of ornament.

2. Fill ornament half full with sugar; replace top securely.

3. Attach name tag to top of ornament with ribbon.

WHAT YOU NEED:

Clear glass ornament

Colored sugar

Name tag

Ribbon

Pear and Blue Cheese Salad

PREP: 20 MINUTES • 12 SERVINGS

Cider Vinaigrette (below)

Romaine leaves

3 red pears, thinly sliced

3 green pears, thinly sliced

3/4 cup crumbled blue cheese

holiday shortcut

Instead of making individual salads, turn this into a tossed salad in a large pretty bowl. Use 12 cups bite-size pieces of romaine, chopped pears, blue cheese and toss with the vinaigrette.

1. Make Cider Vinaigrette.

2. Arrange romaine leaves on 12 salad plates. Divide red and green pear slices evenly among plates. Top each salad with 1 tablespoon blue cheese.

3. Drizzle each salad with about 2 tablespoons vinaigrette.

Cider Vinaigrette

3/4 cup olive or vegetable oil

3 tablespoons cider vinegar

1 1/2 teaspoons Dijon mustard

1/4 teaspoon salt

1/4 teaspoon pepper

Shake all ingredients in tightly covered container.

one serving: Calories 200 (Calories from 145 Fat); Fat 16g; (Saturated 3g); Cholesterol 5mg; Sodium 210mg; Carbohydrate 13g (Dietary Fiber 2g); Protein 3g. % Daily Value: Vitamin A 12%; Vitamin C 16%; Calcium 6%; Iron 2%. Diet Exchanges: 1 Fruit, 3 Fat. Carbohydrate Choices: 1

Cheesy Scalloped Potatoes

PREP: 35 MINUTES • BAKE: 1 HOUR • 12 SERVINGS

4 pounds red potatoes (about 12 medium), cut into 1/4-inch slices

16 ounces process sharp American cheese loaf, diced (4 cups)

1 medium onion, chopped (1/2 cup)

2 teaspoons salt

1/3 cup chopped fresh parsley or 2 tablespoons parsley flakes

1/4 teaspoon pepper

6 tablespoons butter or margarine

1 1/2 cups milk

1/4 cup all-purpose flour

1. Heat oven to 350°. Grease two 2-quart casseroles. In each casserole, layer one-sixth each of the potatoes, cheese, onion, salt, parsley and pepper in casserole. Repeat layers twice. Dot with butter. Mix milk and flour; pour 1/2 of the milk mixture over top of each casserole.

2. Cover and bake 40 minutes. Uncover and bake about 20 minutes longer or until potatoes are tender.

one serving: Calories 320 (Calories from Fat 160); Fat 18g; (Saturated 11g); Cholesterol 55mg; Sodium 990mg; Carbohydrate 30g (Dietary Fiber 3g); Protein 12g. % Daily Value: Vitamin A 18%; Vitamin C 10%; Calcium 24%; Iron 4%. Diet Exchanges: 2 Starch, 1 High-Fat Meat, 1 1/2 Fat. Carbohydrate Choices: 2

holiday shortcut

No time to slice potatoes? Not a problem! Just use two 32-ounce bags of frozen hash brown potatoes instead.

Pine Tree Parmesan Breadsticks

PREP: 15 MINUTES • RISE: 30 MINUTES • BAKE: 15 MINUTES • 12 BREADSTICKS

2 tablespoons olive or vegetable oil

Cornmeal, if desired

12 frozen white bread dough rolls
(from 48-ounce package), thawed

3 or 4 fresh rosemary sprigs

1 tablespoon grated Parmesan cheese

holiday shortcut

Let the kids put in the rosemary and sprinkle on the Parmesan—it's fun for them and less work for you.

1. Brush 2 cookie sheets with olive oil; sprinkle with cornmeal. Roll each ball of dough into 9-inch rope. Place ropes about 1/2 inch apart on cookie sheets.

2. Brush 2 tablespoons oil over dough. Break 36 small clusters of rosemary leaves off rosemary sprigs. Using 3 clusters for each breadstick, insert stem end of each cluster 1/4 inch deep into top of breadstick. Sprinkle cheese over dough. Cover loosely with plastic wrap and let rise in warm place about 30 minutes or until almost double.

3. Heat oven to 350°. Bake 12 to 15 minutes or until light golden brown.

one breadstick: Calories 125 (Calories from Fat 65); Fat 7g; (Saturated 1g); Cholesterol 0mg; Sodium 350mg; Carbohydrate 13g (Dietary Fiber 0g); Protein 2g. % Daily Value: Vitamin A 0%; Vitamin C 0%; Calcium 0%; Iron 4%. Diet Exchanges: 1 Starch, 1 Fat. Carbohydrate Choices: 1

Dark Chocolate Raspberry Fondue

PREP: 15 MINUTES • COOK: 5 MINUTES • 16 SERVINGS (2 TABLESPOONS EACH)

2/3 cup whipping (heavy) cream

1/3 cup seedless raspberry preserves

1 tablespoon honey

1 bag (12 ounces) semisweet chocolate chunks

Assorted dippers (fresh fruit pieces, pretzels, shortbread cookies, pound cake cubes or angel food cake cubes), if desired

holiday shortcut

To save time, use only dippers that don't need to be cut into pieces You may want to try purchased already-cut bite-size pieces of fruit, strawberries, red and green grapes, marshmallows and even ribbed potato chips.

holiday hint

Use special fruits such as fresh figs or pears cut in half lengthwise or cut pound cake with mini star-shaped cookie cutters and purchase pirouette or other fancy cookies for dipping. Place fruits and cookies in pretty cocktail glasses, and arrange with fondue pot on a tray lined with a doily, cheese leaves or parchment paper.

1. Mix whipping cream, raspberry preserves and honey in fondue pot or 2-quart saucepan. Heat over warm/simmer setting or medium-low heat, stirring occasionally, just until bubbles rise to surface (do not boil).

2. Add chocolate; stir with wire whisk until melted. Keep warm over warm/simmer setting. (If using saucepan, pour into fondue pot and keep warm over warm/simmer setting.) Serve with dippers.

one serving: Calories 155 (Calories from Fat 80); Fat 9g; (Saturated 6g); Cholesterol 10mg; Sodium 10mg; Carbohydrate 19g (Dietary Fiber 1g); Protein 1g. % Daily Value: Vitamin A 2%; Vitamin C 0%; Calcium 2%; Iron 4%. Diet Exchanges: 1 Other Carbohydrates, 2 Fat. Carbohydrate Choices: 1

Kid Fun

Take a fun break with the kids! These four pages give you some great ideas to keep Santa's little helpers busy and happy. Everyone knows that Santa looks forward to a snack on his Christmas rounds—it's hard work going up and down chimneys—and these cupcakes and cookies will be very welcome.

Rudolph Cupcakes

24 Cupcakes

WHAT YOU NEED:

1 package cake mix (any non-swirl flavor)

Water, oil and eggs called for on cake mix package

1 tub chocolate ready-to-spread frosting or Creamy Chocolate Frosting

Chocolate sprinkles

24 large pretzel twists

24 miniature marshmallows

12 candied whole cherries

24 red cinnamon candies

HOW TO DO IT:

1. Heat oven to 350°. Bake and cool cake mix as directed on package for cupcakes, using water, oil and eggs.

2. Spread frosting over tops of cupcakes. Sprinkle with chocolate shot.

3. For each cupcake, break pretzel twist in half; arrange on cupcake for reindeer antlers. Cut marshmallow in half; arrange on cupcake for eyes. Cut cherries in half; arrange on cupcake for nose. Place red cinnamon candy below cherry for mouth. Store loosely covered at room temperature.

Cranberry Kissing Ball

No Mistletoe? You can still make merry with this festive kissing ball, using easy-to-find cranberries.

HOW TO DO IT:

1. Wrap wire tightly around diameter of foam ball once. Twist wire at top of ball to secure. Tuck ends into ball.

2. Break toothpicks in half. Push cranberry onto broken end of toothpick; push other end of toothpick into foam ball. Continue until ball is well filled with cranberries.

3. Fill in open spaces on ball with 1 1/2- to 2-inch cuts of eucalyptus, securing with pins.

4. Slip ribbon through wire twist at top; tie ribbon to make loop for hanging ball. The cranberries will stay plump and pretty for about three to four days. To extend its life, hang the ball in a cool spot, such as in an entryway or on a porch.

WHAT YOU NEED:

12 inches 20-gauge wire

1 plastic foam ball, 3 inches in diameter

Round toothpicks

1/2 pound fresh cranberries

1 small bunch (about 5 sprigs) fresh eucalyptus

1 package craft straight pins

1 yard decorative ribbon

Christmas Rainbow Cookies

About 8 Dozen Cookies

WHAT YOU NEED:

Rainbow Dust (below) or purchased colored sugars

2 cups sugar

1 1/2 cups butter or margarine, softened

1 cup flaked coconut

1 teaspoon vanilla

3 cups all-purpose flour

1 teaspoon baking soda

1/2 teaspoon salt

HOW TO DO IT:

1. Prepare Rainbow Dust. Heat oven to 350°

2. Beat 2 cups sugar, the butter, coconut and vanilla in large bowl with electric mixer on medium speed, or mix with spoon. Stir in flour, baking soda and salt.

3. Shape dough by rounded teaspoonfuls into balls. Place about 3 inches apart on ungreased cookie sheet. Press bottom of glass into dough to grease, then dip into Rainbow Dust; press on shaped dough to flatten slightly.

4. Bake 8 to 10 minutes or until edges are golden brown. Remove from cookie sheet to wire rack; cool completely.

Rainbow Dust (Colored Sugar)

Place 1/2 cup sugar in resealable bag. Choose a color from the chart, and add food colors to sugar in bag. Seal bag. Squeeze sugar in bag until it becomes colored. Store sugar in sealed bag or bottle with tight-fitting lid.

COLOR	NUMBER OF DROPS OF LIQUID FOOD COLOR
Orange	2 drops yellow and 2 drops red
Peach	4 drops yellow and 1 drop red
Yellow	4 drops yellow
Pale yellow	2 drops yellow
Green	8 drops green
Lime Green	3 drops yellow and 1 drop green
Blue	5 drops blue
Turquoise Blue	3 drops blue and 1 drop green
Baby Blue	2 drops blue
Purple	3 drops red and 2 drops blue
Red	10 drops red
Rose	5 drops red and 1 drop blue
Pink	1 drop red

CHRISTMAS OPEN HOUSE

SERVES 12 TO 15

*Roasted Vegetable Lasagna

*Baked Spinach, Crab and Artichoke Dip

*Festive Cheese Trio

*Fruit Kabobs with Tropical Fruit Coulis

Baby Carrots and Your Favorite Store-Bought Dip

*Christmas Tree Appetizers

or

Olive Tapenade*

*Roasted Sesame and Honey Snack Mix

or

*Savory Pecans

*Strawberry Santas

*Luscious Chocolate Truffles

*RECIPES FOLLOW

Roasted Vegetable Lasagna

PREP: 25 MINUTES • BAKE: 1 HOUR 15 MINUTES • STAND: 5 MINUTES • 8 SERVINGS

2 medium red, green or yellow bell peppers, each cut into 8 pieces

1 medium onion, cut into 8 wedges

1 large zucchini, cut into 2-inch pieces (2 cups)

6 small red potatoes, cut into fourths

1 package (8 ounces) whole mushrooms, cut in half

2 tablespoons olive or vegetable oil

1/2 teaspoon peppered seasoned salt

2 teaspoons chopped fresh or 1/2 teaspoon dried basil leaves

9 uncooked lasagna noodles (9 ounces)

1 container (15 ounces) ricotta cheese

1/2 cup basil pesto

1 egg, slightly beaten

2 cups shredded provolone cheese (8 ounces)

1 cup shredded mozzarella cheese (4 ounces)

1. Heat oven to 425°. Spray bottom and sides of jelly roll pan, 15 1/2 × 10 1/2 × 1 inch, with cooking spray. Place bell peppers, onion, zucchini, potatoes, mushrooms, oil, peppered seasoned salt and basil in large bowl; toss to coat. Spread vegetables in pan. Bake uncovered about 30 minutes or until crisp-tender. Cool slightly.

2. Reduce oven temperature to 350°. Spray bottom and sides of rectangular baking dish, 13 × 9 × 2 inches, with cooking spray. Cook and drain noodles as directed on package. Mix ricotta cheese, pesto and egg. Coarsely chop vegetables.

3. Place 3 noodles lengthwise in baking dish. Spread with half of the ricotta mixture. Top with 2 cups vegetables and 1 cup of the provolone cheese. Repeat layers, starting with noodles. Top with remaining 3 noodles and remaining vegetables. Sprinkle with mozzarella cheese.

4. Bake uncovered 40 to 45 minutes or until hot in center and top is golden brown. Let stand 5 minutes before cutting.

one serving: Calories 495 (Calories from Fat 245); Fat 27g; (Saturated 11g); Cholesterol 75mg; Sodium 630mg; Carbohydrate 42g (Dietary Fiber 5g); Protein 26g. % Daily Value: Vitamin A 56%; Vitamin C 60%; Calcium 56%; Iron 20%. Diet Exchanges: 2 Starches, 2 Vegetables, 2 High-Fat Meat, 2 Fat. Carbohydrate Choices: 3

holiday DO-AHEAD *tip*

Roasting vegetables takes some time, but the richly flavored results are definitely worth it. To get a jump start, roast vegetables up to 8 hours in advance and refrigerate.

Baked Spinach, Crab and Artichoke Dip

PREP: 10 MINUTES • BAKE: 20 MINUTES • 24 SERVINGS (2 TABLESPOONS EACH)

1 cup mayonnaise or salad dressing

1 cup freshly grated Parmesan cheese

1 can (14 ounces) artichoke hearts, drained and coarsely chopped

1 package (10 ounces) frozen chopped spinach, thawed and squeezed to drain

1 package (8 ounces) refrigerated imitation crabmeat chunks

1 cup shredded Monterey Jack or Cheddar cheese (4 ounces)

Toasted baguette slices or assorted crackers, if desired

holiday FLAVOR *twist*

If you prefer fresh spinach, use one cup of loosely packed, coarsely chopped spinach leaves for the frozen spinach.

holiday DO-AHEAD *tip*

This sensational, simple-to-prepare dip can be made and refrigerated before baking up to 24 hours ahead. Bake as directed.

1. Heat oven to 350°. Mix mayonnaise and Parmesan cheese in medium bowl. Stir in artichoke hearts, spinach and crabmeat.

2. Spoon mixture into 1-quart casserole. Sprinkle with Monterey Jack cheese.

3. Cover and bake 15 to 20 minutes or until cheese is melted. Serve warm with baguette slices.

one serving: Calories 120 (Calories from Fat 90); Fat 10g; (Saturated 3g); Cholesterol 15mg; Sodium 290mg; Carbohydrate 3g (Dietary Fiber 1g); Protein 5g. % Daily Value: Vitamin A 8%; Vitamin C 2%; Calcium 10%; Iron 2%. Diet Exchanges: 1/2 Lean Meat, 2 Fat. Carbohydrate Choices: 0

Festive Cheese Trio

PREP: 45 MINUTES • CHILL: 24 HOURS • 16 SERVINGS (2 TABLESPOONS EACH)

1 package (8 ounces) cream cheese, softened

1 package (3 ounces) cream cheese, softened

1 package (6 ounces) chèvre (goat) cheese

1 1/2 tablespoons chopped fresh chives

2 tablespoons finely chopped yellow bell pepper

2 tablespoons finely chopped walnuts, toasted

2 tablespoons chopped pitted Kalamata or Spanish olives

2 tablespoons freshly grated Parmesan cheese

1 jar (2 ounces) diced pimientos, drained

Crackers or cocktail breads, if desired

1. Line three 6-ounce custard cups or molds with plastic wrap. Beat cream cheese and chèvre cheese with electric mixer on medium speed until smooth. Divide mixture into three equal portions (about 2/3 cup each).

2. Stir chives into one portion of cheese mixture. Spoon half of mixture evenly into a lined cup. Sprinkle with bell pepper. Top with remaining chives mixture. Cover and refrigerate at least 24 hours but no longer than 3 days.

3. Stir walnuts into another portion of cheese mixture. Spoon half of mixture evenly into a lined cup. Top with olives. Top with remaining walnut mixture. Cover and refrigerate at least 24 hours but no longer than 3 days.

4. Stir Parmesan cheese into remaining portion of cheese mixture. Spoon half of mixture evenly into remaining lined cup. Top with pimientos. Top with remaining Parmesan mixture. Cover and refrigerate at least 24 hours but no longer than 3 days.

5. Turn cups upside down onto serving plate; carefully remove cups and plastic wrap from cheese mixtures. Serve with crackers.

one serving: Calories 110 (Calories from Fat 90); Fat 10g; (Saturated 6g); Cholesterol 30mg; Sodium 200mg; Carbohydrate 1g (Dietary Fiber 0g); Protein 4g. % Daily Value: Vitamin A 8%; Vitamin C 8%; Calcium 8%; Iron 2%. Diet Exchanges: 1 Medium-Fat Meat, 1 Fat. Carbohydrate Choices: 0

holiday hint

Make little flags to insert into the tops of the unmolded spreads that identify the flavors of each cheese. Place cheese spreads in a row on long narrow platter (about 12 × 5 inches). Garnish with edible white flowers.

A Toast to Beverages

Jazz up liquid refreshments at holiday gatherings with these indispensable ideas. Whether you're serving coffee, cocktails or wine, just follow your taste buds and add a splash of creativity for out-standing holiday drinks!

Hot Stuff

Tradition. Comfort. What better words to describe a cup of hot coffee or a mug of steaming cocoa? Add a contemporary twist to these favorites with these ideas:

To coffee, stir in about 1 tablespoon chocolate syrup, crème de cacao, hazelnut liqueur or syrup, caramel topping or a small scoop of your favorite ice cream.

Add pieces of vanilla bean, a cardamom pod and/or cinnamon stick to a pot or cups of coffee or hot chocolate for a spicy flavor and aroma.

To hot chocolate, add about 1 tablespoon crème de menthe, orange-flavored liqueur, cherry syrup, coffee liqueur or syrup, caramel topping, toasted coconut or a small scoop of your favorite ice cream.

A Twist on Beer

Enjoying a cold beer while mowing the lawn or listening to the ball game is great. But when the holidays roll around, it's fun to jazz up beer.

To a tall glass of beer, add a shot (1 to 2 ounces) of whiskey, gin or vodka.

Spike a full glass of beer with a couple tablespoons of lemon or lime juice. Start with a small amount, and add more if you like.

Mix equal parts of chilled beer and either chilled tomato juice, ginger ale or orange juice for a colorful, flavorful beer drink.

Drink Dazzlers for Beer

Use celery stalks as stirrers.

Add lemon, lime or orange slices to glasses.

Drink Dazzlers for Hot Beverages

Drizzle chocolate syrup inside glass (use a small squeeze bottle or spoon).

Use a vanilla bean pod, cinnamon stick or peppermint stick as a stirrer.

Top with whipped cream, and garnish with chocolate-covered coffee beans, shaved chocolate, chopped nuts, chocolate chips or crushed candies or cookies. Or drizzle with crème de menthe, cherry syrup or maple syrup.

Flavor your sweetened whipped cream with 1 to 2 tablespoons cocoa, spices (ground cinnamon, nutmeg or even a pinch of ground red pepper), ground nuts, crushed peppermint or a small amount of flavored liqueur.

Dust the top of your drink with cocoa, cinnamon or nutmeg. Or sprinkle with toasted coconut.

Fine Wines

Wine is a year-round favorite. Enjoy it served straight from the bottle, or embellish it with fun results.

To enjoy "wine coolers," mix equal parts of white wine and fruit juice. You can also add a shot of fruit-flavored liqueur if you like.

Add honey and spices such as cinnamon, cardamom and cloves to red wine, then heat slowly for a mulled wine.

Holiday Spritzer

Make a pretty wine spritzer—it's so easy and refreshing during the holidays.

Mix 2 cups chilled dry white wine, nonalcoholic wine or apple juice; 1 cup chilled cran-apple juice cocktail and 1 cup chilled sparkling water. Serve over ice and garnish with apple slices and mint leaves if desired. This will make six 3/4-cup servings.

Spirited Drinks

Spiked gelatin cubes, with their colorful, wiggly shapes and dazzling flavors, are the rage.

Prepare any 4-serving-size package of flavored gelatin using 1 cup boiling water.

After the gelatin is dissolved, stir in 3/4 cup of your favorite spirit, perhaps rum, brandy, vodka, gin or champagne. Spray ice-cube trays with cooking spray. Pour gelatin mixture into ice-cube trays and refrigerate until set. Remove from the trays, and serve the cubes in small glasses.

A Classic Cocktail

Imbued with nostalgia and romance, the martini holds a certain place of honor with those who enjoy cocktails. As a result, this simple, sophisticated drink is popular again.

A traditional dry martini is 1 1/2 to 2 ounces of gin with a splash (about 2 teaspoons) of dry vermouth. It is shaken (or stirred, if you prefer) with ice to make it refreshingly cold. The ice is strained, and an olive or two added. The less vermouth a martini has, the "drier" it is. Be sure to chill the martini glasses or add ice while making the martinis (and then remove before serving).

Those with adventurous palates have expanded on the classic and created Vodka Martinis (substitute vodka for the gin), Cosmopolitans (vodka with orange-flavored liqueur, cranberry juice and line juice), Mintinis (substitute white crème de menthe for the vermouth) and Tequinis (substitute tequila for the gin).

Drink Dazzlers for Mixed Drinks

Glass rims can be rubbed with the cut side of a lime or lemon and then dipped into salt or sugar. Spice the salt or sugar, or use colored sugar crystals for a fun touch.

Make ice cubes out of juices for a colorful effect: cranberry juice for red cubes, grape juice for purple cubes and mango juice for yellow.

Instead of the traditional olive garnish, try a fruit garnish. Use fresh berries, cherries, citrus twists, kiwifruit slice or melon wedges.

Fruit Kabobs with Tropical Fruit Coulis

PREP: 40 MINUTES • 24 APPETIZERS

6 cups bite-size pieces assorted fresh fruit (pineapple, watermelon and cantaloupe)

1 cup green grapes

1 cup blueberries or red grapes

3 small starfruit, cut into 24 slices

2 large mangoes, peeled, seeds removed and cut into large pieces

1/4 cup pineapple preserves

holiday *shortcut*

Instead of making kabobs, serve fruit in a large glass bowl with the coulis in a separate bowl. Include toothpicks, and let guests help themselves.

holiday FLAVOR *twist*

Cut the watermelon with mini star-shaped cookie cutters. Place skewers in a clear glass vase. Or cut a fresh pineapple (including top) lengthwise in half. Place pineapple on serving platter, and insert skewers into pineapple. Serve coulis in a pretty cocktail glass.

1. Thread 4 to 6 pieces of fruits (except mangoes) on each of twenty-four 6-inch skewers. Place skewers on large serving platter; set aside.

2. Place mango pieces and pineapple preserves in food processor. Cover and process until smooth; pour into small serving bowl. Serve kabobs with mango coulis.

one appetizer: Calories 50 (Calories from Fat 0); Fat 0g; (Saturated 0g); Cholesterol 0mg; Sodium 5mg; Carbohydrate 12g (Dietary Fiber 1g); Protein 0g. % Daily Value: Vitamin A 12%; Vitamin C 30%; Calcium 0%; Iron 0%. Diet Exchanges: 1 Fruit. Carbohydrate Choices: 1

Christmas Tree Appetizers

PREP: 20 MINUTES • CHILL: 2 HOURS • 64 APPETIZERS

1 package (8 ounces) cream cheese, softened

1/2 cup chopped drained roasted red bell peppers (from 7-ounce jar)

1/4 cup chopped ripe olives

1/4 cup chopped fresh basil leaves

1/4 cup shredded Parmesan cheese

4 spinach-flavor flour tortillas (8 to 10 inches in diameter)

Ripe olive pieces

holiday shortcut

Want to save some time? Skip pressing into the shape of Christmas trees, and just prepare the filing as directed. Spread on tortillas and roll up. Refrigerate 2 hours, and cut into slices.

1. Mix all ingredients except tortillas and olive pieces. Divide mixture among tortillas, spreading to edges of tortillas. Roll up tightly. Press each tortilla roll into triangle shape, using fingers. Wrap in plastic wrap. Refrigerate at least 2 hours but no longer than 24 hours.

2. To serve, cut rolls into 1/2-inch slices. Place olive piece at bottom of each triangle to look like a tree trunk; secure with toothpick.

one appetizer: Calories 30 (Calories from Fat 20); Fat 2g; (Saturated 1g); Cholesterol 5mg; Sodium 40mg; Carbohydrate 2g (Dietary Fiber 0g); Protein 1g. % Daily Value: Vitamin A 2%; Vitamin C 4%; Calcium 0%; Iron 0%. Diet Exchanges: 1/2 Fat. Carbohydrate Choices: 0

Roasted Sesame and Honey Snack Mix

PREP: 10 MINUTES • BAKE: 45 MINUTES • COOL: 30 MINUTES • 20 SERVINGS (1/2 CUP EACH)

3 cups Chex® cereal (any variety)

3 cups checkerboard-shaped pretzels

3 cups sesame sticks

1 cup mixed nuts

1/4 cup honey

3 tablespoons butter or margarine, melted

2 tablespoons sesame seed, toasted, if desired

holiday tip
DO-AHEAD

To ease the load of last-minute preparation, make this snack mix up to 1 week ahead and store in an airtight container.

1. Heat oven to 275°. Mix cereal, pretzels, sesame sticks and nuts in ungreased jelly roll pan, 15 1/2 × 10 1/2 × 1 inch.

2. Mix remaining ingredients. Pour over cereal mixture, stirring until evenly coated.

3. Bake 45 minutes, stirring occasionally. Spread on waxed paper; cool.

one serving: Calories 215 (Calories from Fat 80); Fat 9g; (Saturated 2g); Cholesterol 5mg; Sodium 530mg; Carbohydrate 30g (Dietary Fiber 2g); Protein 4g. % Daily Value: Vitamin A 2%; Vitamin C 0%; Calcium 2%; Iron 4%. Diet Exchanges: 1 Starch, 1 Other Carbohydrates, 1 1/2 Fat. Carbohydrate Choices: 2

Savory Pecans

PREP: 5 MINUTES • BAKE: 10 MINUTES • 8 SERVINGS (1/4 CUP EACH)

2 cups pecan halves

2 medium green onions, chopped
(2 tablespoons)

2 tablespoons butter or margarine, melted

1 tablespoon soy sauce

1/4 teaspoon ground red pepper (cayenne)

1. Heat oven to 300°. Mix all ingredients. Spread pecans in single layer in ungreased jelly roll pan, 15 1/2 × 10 1/2 × 1 inch.

2. Bake uncovered about 10 minutes or until pecans are toasted. Serve warm, or cool completely. Store in airtight container at room temperature up to 3 weeks.

one serving: Calories 225 (Calories from Fat 200); Fat 22g; (Saturated 3g); Cholesterol 10mg; Sodium 135mg; Carbohydrate 4g (Dietary Fiber 3g); Protein 3g. % Daily Value: Vitamin A 2%; Vitamin C 0%; Calcium 2%; Iron 4%. Diet Exchanges: 1/2 High-Fat Meat, 4 Fat. Carbohydrate Choices: 0

holiday
FLAVOR *twist*

For ***Chinese-spiced pecans***, omit the ground red pepper and stir in 2 teaspoons five-spice powder and 1/2 teaspoon ground ginger.

For ***Tex-Mex pecans***, omit soy sauce and ground red pepper and stir in 1 tablespoon Worcestershire sauce, 2 teaspoons chili powder, 1/4 teaspoon garlic salt and 1/4 teaspoon onion powder.

Strawberry Santas

PREP: 30 MINUTES • 12 SANTAS

1 package (8 ounces) cream cheese, softened

1/2 cup marshmallow creme

12 large strawberries

12 fresh or canned pineapple chunks
(1-inch pieces)

12 frilled toothpicks

24 miniature semisweet chocolate chips

12 white chocolate–covered creme-filled
chocolate sandwich cookies

holiday tip
DO-AHEAD

Have the kids assemble these charming Santas the morning of the party—they'll be busy while you pull together the rest of the party. Don't make them the night before—they shouldn't be in the refrigerator longer than 2 hours.

1. Beat cream cheese and marshmallow creme in medium bowl with electric mixture on high speed until fluffy. Place cream cheese mixture in decorating bag fitted with #17 star tip or in resealable plastic food bag.

2. Cut strawberries crosswise in half. Thread strawberry piece, pineapple chunk and remaining strawberry piece onto toothpick; press chocolate chips into pineapple for eyes. Pipe cream cheese mixture onto strawberry "hat" to form fur trim and onto pineapple to form beard. (If using bag, snip corner of bag to pipe cream cheese.) Cover and refrigerate no longer than 2 hours. Serve on sandwich cookies.

one santa: Calories 95 (Calories from Fat 65); Fat 7g; (Saturated 4g); Cholesterol 20mg; Sodium 60mg; Carbohydrate 7g (Dietary Fiber 1g); Protein 2g. % Daily Value: Vitamin A 6%; Vitamin C 20%; Calcium 2%; Iron 2%. Diet Exchanges: 1/2 Fruit, 1 Fat. Carbohydrate Choices: 1/2

Luscious Chocolate Truffles

PREP: 20 MINUTES • CHILL: 25 MINUTES • FREEZE: 30 MINUTES • ABOUT 15 TRUFFLES

1 bag (12 ounces) semisweet chocolate chips (2 cups)

2 tablespoons butter or margarine

1/4 cup whipping (heavy) cream

2 tablespoons liqueur (almond, cherry, coffee, hazelnut, Irish cream, orange, raspberry, etc.), if desired

1 tablespoon shortening

Finely chopped nuts, if desired

Finely chopped dried apricots, if desired

White baking bar, chopped, if desired

holiday
DO-AHEAD *tip*

You can make these delightful truffles up to a week ahead—just take then out of the frige about half an hour before serving because the flavor and texture is better.

1. Line cookie sheet with aluminum foil or parchment paper. Melt 1 cup of the chocolate chips in heavy 2-quart saucepan over low heat, stirring constantly; remove from heat. Stir in butter. Stir in whipping cream and liqueur. Refrigerate 10 to 15 minutes, stirring frequently, just until thick enough to hold a shape.

2. Drop mixture by teaspoonfuls onto cookie sheet. Shape into balls. (If mixture is too sticky, refrigerate until firm enough to shape.) Freeze 30 minutes.

3. Heat shortening and remaining 1 cup chocolate chips over low heat, stirring constantly, until chocolate is melted and mixture is smooth; remove from heat. Dip truffles, one at a time, into chocolate. Return to cookie sheet. Immediately sprinkle nuts and apricots over some of the truffles. Refrigerate 10 minutes or until coating is set.

4. Heat baking bar over low heat, stirring constantly, until melted. Drizzle over some of the truffles. Refrigerate just until set. Store in airtight container in refrigerator. Remove truffles from refrigerator about 30 minutes before serving; serve at room temperature.

one truffle: Calories 145 (Calories from Fat 90); Fat 10g; (Saturated 6g); Cholesterol 10mg; Sodium 15mg; Carbohydrate 14g (Dietary Fiber 1g); Protein 1g. % Daily Value: Vitamin A 2%; Vitamin C 0%; Calcium 0%; Iron 4%. Diet Exchanges: 1 Other Carbohydrates, 2 Fat. Carbohydrate Choices: 1

Olive Tapenade

PREP: 10 MINUTES • 14 SERVINGS (2 TABLESPOONS EACH)

1 1/2 cups pitted Kalamata or ripe olives

1/4 cup chopped walnuts

3 tablespoons olive or vegetable oil

3 tablespoons capers, drained

1 1/2 teaspoons fresh rosemary leaves

1 teaspoon Italian seasoning

2 cloves garlic

Chopped red bell pepper, if desired

Assorted crackers, if desired

holiday tip
DO-AHEAD

Go ahead and make this savory spread up to 2 days ahead—just refrigerate until ready to serve.

1. Place all ingredients except bell pepper and crackers in food processor or blender. Cover and process, using quick on-and-off motions, until slightly coarse.

2. Spoon into serving dish. Sprinkle with bell pepper. Serve with crackers.

one serving: Calories 60 (Calories from Fat 55); Fat 6g; (Saturated 1g); Cholesterol 0mg; Sodium 180mg; Carbohydrate 2g (Dietary Fiber 1g); Protein 1g. % Daily Value: Vitamin A 2%; Vitamin C 4%; Calcium 2%; Iron 2%. Diet Exchanges: 1 Fat. Carbohydrate Choices: 0

KWANZAA

BEGINNING DECEMBER 26 and wrapping up January 1,
Kwanzaa, the newest of our holidays, celebrates African-
American culture. Created in 1966 by Dr. Maulana Karenga,
a teacher and civil rights leader, "Kwanzaa" means "first
fruits" in Swahili. The holiday serves to reinforce and build
family, culture and community. Each of the holiday's seven
nights focuses on a different basic principle: unity, self-deter-
mination, collective work and responsibility, cooperative
economics, purpose, creativity and faith. Gather your friends
and family together over this Kwanzaa feast to pay tribute to
the values you hold most dear.

KWANZAA FEAST

SERVES 6

*Buttered Rum-Spiced Cider

*Moroccan Chicken with Olives

*Shrimp Gumbo

*African Squash and Yams

*Hot and Spicy Greens

*Tropical Fruit Salad

*Cheddar Cheese Biscuits

*Sweet Potato Cake

*RECIPE FOLLOWS

Buttered Rum-Spiced Cider

PREP: 10 MINUTES • COOK: 15 MINUTES • 6 SERVINGS (1 CUP EACH)

6 cups apple cider

1/2 teaspoon whole cloves

1/4 teaspoon ground nutmeg

3 sticks cinnamon

6 tablespoons butter (do not use margarine because it will separate)

6 tablespoons packed brown sugar

3/4 cup rum

1. Heat cider, cloves, nutmeg and cinnamon to boiling in 3-quart saucepan over medium-high heat; reduce heat to low. Simmer uncovered 10 minutes. Strain cider mixture to remove cloves and cinnamon if desired.

2. For each serving, place 1 tablespoon butter, 1 tablespoon brown sugar and 2 tablespoons rum in mug. Fill with hot cider.

one serving: Calories 275 (Calories from Fat 110); Fat 12g (Saturated 7g); Cholesterol 30mg; Sodium 90mg; Carbohydrate 42g (Dietary Fiber 0g); Protein 0g. % Daily Value: Vitamin A 10%; Vitamin C 2%; Calcium 2%; Iron 6%. Diet Exchanges: 2 Fruit, 1 Other Carbohydrates, 2 Fat. Carbohydrate Choices: 3

holiday FLAVOR *twist*

Prefer spiced cider? Just prepare as directed above except omit the butter, brown sugar and rum.

Moroccan Chicken with Olives

PREP: 25 MINUTES • BAKE: 1 HOUR • 6 SERVINGS

1/4 cup chopped fresh cilantro	1/3 cup all-purpose flour
1 tablespoon paprika	1/2 cup water
2 teaspoons ground cumin	1/4 cup lemon juice
1/2 teaspoon salt	1 teaspoon chicken bouillon granules
1/2 teaspoon ground turmeric	1/2 cup pitted Kalamata or Greek olives
1/2 teaspoon ground ginger	1 medium lemon, sliced
2 cloves garlic, finely chopped	Hot cooked couscous, if desired
3- to 3 1/2-pound cut-up broiler-fryer chicken	

holiday history

The *mkeke*, or straw mat, that is used during Kwanzaa reminds people of the beautiful woven straw baskets and mats of Africa. You might want to serve this North African dish on a straw mat and slip the bowl of couscous into a colorful basket in honor of African traditions.

1. Heat oven to 350°.

2. Mix cilantro, paprika, cumin, salt, turmeric, ginger and garlic. Rub cilantro mixture on all sides of chicken; coat chicken with flour. Place chicken in ungreased rectangular baking dish, 13 × 9 × 2 inches. Mix water, lemon juice and bouillon granules; pour over chicken. Add olives and lemon slices.

3. Bake uncovered about 1 hour, spooning juices over chicken occasionally, until juice of chicken is no longer pink when centers of thickest pieces are cut. Serve with couscous.

one serving: Calories 275 (Calories from Fat 135); Fat 15g; (Saturated 4g); Cholesterol 85mg; Sodium 600mg; Carbohydrate 7g (Dietary Fiber 1g); Protein 28g. % Daily Value: Vitamin A 2%; Vitamin C 2%; Calcium 2%; Iron 10%. Diet Exchanges: 1/2 Starch, 4 Lean Meat, 1/2 Fat. Carbohydrate Choices: 1/2

Shrimp Gumbo

PREP: 20 MINUTES • COOK: 1 HOUR • 6 SERVINGS

1/4 cup butter or margarine

2 medium onions, sliced

1 medium green bell pepper, cut into thin strips

2 cloves garlic, finely chopped

2 tablespoons all-purpose flour

3 cups beef broth

1/2 teaspoon red pepper sauce

1/4 teaspoon salt

1/4 teaspoon pepper

1 bay leaf

1 package (10 ounces) frozen cut okra, thawed

1 can (14 1/2 ounces) whole tomatoes, undrained

1 can (6 ounces) tomato paste

1 1/2 pounds uncooked fresh or frozen medium shrimp in shells

Hot cooked rice, if desired

1/4 cup chopped fresh parsley, if desired

holiday shortcut

In a time bind? Use 1 pound frozen uncooked peeled deveined medium shrimp, for the 1 1/2 pounds shrimp in shells.

1. Melt butter in 4-quart Dutch oven over medium heat. Cook onions, bell pepper and garlic in butter 5 minutes, stirring occasionally. Stir in flour. Cook over medium heat, stirring constantly, until bubbly; remove from heat.

2. Stir in remaining ingredients except shrimp, rice and parsley, breaking up tomatoes with a fork or snipping with kitchen scissors. Heat to boiling; reduce heat. Simmer uncovered 45 minutes, stirring occasionally.

3. Peel shrimp. (If shrimp are frozen, do not thaw; peel in cold water.) Make a shallow cut lengthwise down back of each shrimp; wash out vein.

4. Stir shrimp into gumbo. Cover and simmer about 5 minutes or until shrimp are pink and firm. Remove bay leaf. Serve in bowls over rice and sprinkle with parsley.

one serving: Calories 215 (Calories from Fat 80); Fat 9g (Saturated 5g); Cholesterol 125mg; Sodium 1120mg; Carbohydrate 18g (Dietary Fiber 4g); Protein 16g. % Daily Value: Vitamin A 30%; Vitamin C 40%; Calcium 10%; Iron 18%. Diet Exchanges: 1/2 Starch, 2 Vegetable, 1 1/2 Lean Meat. Carbohydrate Choices: 1

African Squash and Yams

PREP: 10 MINUTES • COOK: 20 MINUTES • 6 SERVINGS

2 tablespoons vegetable oil

1 small onion, chopped (1/4 cup)

1 pound Hubbard squash, peeled and cut into 1-inch pieces

2 medium yams or sweet potatoes (3/4 pound), peeled and cut into 1-inch pieces

1 cup canned coconut milk

1/2 teaspoon salt

1/2 teaspoon ground cinnamon

1/4 teaspoon ground cloves

1. Heat oil in 10-inch skillet over medium heat. Cook onion in oil about 5 minutes, stirring occasionally, until tender.

2. Stir in remaining ingredients. Heat to boiling; reduce heat. Cover and simmer 10 minutes. Simmer uncovered about 5 minutes longer, stirring occasionally, until vegetables are tender.

one serving: Calories 195 (Calories from Fat 110); Fat 12g; (Saturated 7g); Cholesterol 0mg; Sodium 220mg; Carbohydrate 19g (Dietary Fiber 4g); Protein 3g. % Daily Value: Vitamin A 100%; Vitamin C 10%; Calcium 2%; Iron 4%. Diet Exchanges: 1 Starch, 1 Vegetable, 2 Fat. Carbohydrate Choices: 1

holiday history

Kwanzaa means "first fruits," so foods of the harvest are served. Yams are popular in parts of Africa, and when partnered with squash, make a delicious dish to celebrate this season.

Hot and Spicy Greens

PREP: 10 MINUTES • COOK: 10 MINUTES • 6 SERVINGS

2 tablespoons butter or margarine

2 pounds collard greens, coarsely chopped

1 serrano chili, seeded and finely chopped

2 tablespoons finely chopped onion

1 to 2 teaspoons grated gingerroot

holiday FLAVOR *twist*

Folks in your family not fans of collards? Use 2 pounds fresh spinach, chopped, instead. And if they prefer it a little less "hot," reduce the amount of chili.

1. Melt butter in Dutch oven over medium heat.

2. Cook greens, chili, onion and gingerroot in butter about 8 to 10 minutes, stirring frequently, until onion and greens are tender; drain.

one serving: Calories 75 (Calories from Fat 35); Fat 4g; (Saturated 2g); Cholesterol 10mg; Sodium 50mg; Carbohydrate 7g (Dietary Fiber 4g); Protein 3g. % Daily Value: Vitamin A 100%; Vitamin C 48%; Calcium 16%; Iron 2%. Diet Exchanges: 1 Vegetable, 1 Fat. Carbohydrate Choices: 1/2

Tropical Fruit Salad

PREP: 30 MINUTES • CHILL: 1 HOUR • 8 SERVINGS

Almond Dressing (below)

3 bananas, peeled and sliced

2 avocados, peeled, pitted and sliced

2 kiwifruit, peeled and sliced

1 mango, cut lengthwise in half, pitted and cut up

1 papaya, peeled, seeded and sliced

1/4 cup flaked coconut, toasted*

1. Make Almond Dressing.

2. Carefully mix remaining ingredients except coconut in large bowl. Just before serving, sprinkle with coconut. Serve with dressing.

holiday FLAVOR *twist*

If you don't care to use rum in the dressing, just use an additional 2 tablespoons of orange juice instead.

Almond Dressing

1/3 cup chopped almonds, toasted**

1/3 cup orange juice

1/3 cup vegetable oil

3 tablespoons packed brown sugar

2 tablespoons light rum

1/4 teaspoon salt

1/4 teaspoon paprika

Shake all ingredients in tightly covered container. Refrigerate at least 1 hour.

*To toast coconut, spread evenly on ungreased cookie sheet and bake in 350° oven 5 to 7 minutes, stirring occasionally, until golden brown.

**To toast almonds, spread evenly in ungreased shallow pan and bake in 350° oven about 10 minutes, stirring occasionally, until golden brown.

one serving: Calories 310 (Calories from Fat 180); Fat 20g (Saturated 3g); Cholesterol 0mg; Sodium 90mg; Carbohydrate 33g (Dietary Fiber 6g); Protein 3g. % Daily Value: Vitamin A 14%; Vitamin C 100%; Calcium 4%; Iron 6%. Diet Exchanges: 2 Fruit, 4 Fat. Carbohydrate Choices: 2

Nature's Bounty Centerpiece

Kwanzaa is based on African holidays that honor the gathering of the harvest. Although December and January are not harvest months for many of us, there are still many seasonal fruits, vegetables and flowers to use in this centerpiece. You can make your selection based on the Kwanzaa colors: black, red and green.

WHAT YOU NEED:

8-inch grapevine wreath

6-inch piece of wire or twist-tie

Assorted fresh fruits and vegetables

Fresh flowers in water tubes

Fresh bay leaves cut into 6-inch sections or other leaves

Votive candles in candleholders

HOW TO DO IT:

1. Unwind grapevine wreath and fan out to form figure-eight shape. Wrap wire around center to secure. Place on table or large tray.

2. Cluster some fruits, vegetables and flowers in center of grapevine. Arrange additional pieces around outside of centerpiece. Add bay leaves to fill in spaces.

3. Place candles in the clusters, throughout the grapevine and around outside of centerpiece.

Cheddar Cheese Biscuits

PREP: 10 MINUTES • BAKE: 10 MINUTES • 10–12 BISCUITS

2 cups Original Bisquick mix

2/3 cup milk

1/2 cup shredded Cheddar cheese (2 ounces)

1/4 cup butter or margarine, melted

1/4 teaspoon garlic powder, if desired

holiday FLAVOR twist

Adding herbs gives you a whole new biscuit treat. You can stir in 3/4 teaspoon dried dill weed, crumbled dried rosemary leaves or Italian seasoning with the Bisquick.

1. Heat oven to 450°. Mix Bisquick mix, milk and cheese until soft dough forms; beat vigorously 30 seconds. Drop dough by 10 to 12 spoonfuls about 2 inches apart onto ungreased cookie sheet.

2. Bake 8 to 10 minutes or until golden brown. Mix butter and garlic powder; brush on warm biscuits before removing from cookie sheet. Serve warm.

one biscuit: Calories 165 (Calories from Fat 80); Fat 9g; (Saturated 5g); Cholesterol 20mg; Sodium 420mg; Carbohydrate 15g (Dietary Fiber 0g); Protein 4g. % Daily Value: Vitamin A 4%; Vitamin C 0%; Calcium 8%; Iron 4%. Diet Exchanges: 1 Starch, 2 Fat. Carbohydrate Choices: 1

Sweet Potato Cake

PREP: 20 MINUTES • BAKE: 50 MINUTES • COOL: 2 HOURS 10 MINUTES • 16 SERVINGS

2 1/3 cups all-purpose flour

1 1/2 cups sugar

3/4 teaspoon baking soda

1/2 teaspoon baking powder

1/2 teaspoon salt

3/4 cup mashed cooked or canned sweet potatoes

2/3 cup sour cream

1/2 cup plain yogurt

1/2 cup butter or margarine, softened

1 teaspoon vanilla

3 egg yolks

1/3 cup chopped pecans

holiday tip
DO-AHEAD

You can freeze this tasty cake up to 2 months before the celebration. After the cake is completely cool, wrap it tightly in heavy-duty aluminum foil or plastic wrap and pop it in the freezer. About 4 hours before serving, thaw it, wrapped, at room temperature. Give it a fresh sprinkle of powdered sugar before serving.

1. Heat oven to 350°. Grease and flour 12-cup bundt cake pan or angel food cake pan (tube pan), 10 × 4 inches.

2. Stir together flour, sugar, baking soda, baking powder and salt in medium bowl; set aside.

3. Beat sweet potatoes, sour cream, yogurt, butter, vanilla and egg yolks in large bowl on medium speed until blended. Beat in flour mixture; beat 2 minutes. Stir in pecans. Spoon into pan.

4. Bake 45 to 50 minutes or until toothpick inserted in center comes out clean. Cool 10 minutes. Remove from pan; cool completely. Sprinkle with powdered sugar if desired.

one serving: Calories 265 (Calories from Fat 100); Fat 11g (Saturated 5g); Cholesterol 60mg; Sodium 200mg; Carbohydrate 37g (Dietary Fiber 1g); Protein 4g. % Daily Value: Vitamin A 42%; Vitamin C 2%; Calcium 4%; Iron 6%. Diet Exchanges: 1 1/2 Starch, 1 Other Carbohydrates, 2 Fat. Carbohydrate Choices: 2 1/2

Metric Conversion Guide

Volume

U.S. Units	Canadian Metric	Australian Metric
1/4 teaspoon	1 mL	1 ml
1/2 teaspoon	2 mL	2 ml
1 teaspoon	5 mL	5 ml
1 tablespoon	15 mL	20 ml
1/4 cup	50 mL	60 ml
1/3 cup	75 mL	80 ml
1/2 cup	125 mL	125 ml
2/3 cup	150 mL	170 ml
3/4 cup	175 mL	190 ml
1 cup	250 mL	250 ml
1 quart	1 liter	1 liter
1 1/2 quarts	1.5 liters	1.5 liters
2 quarts	2 liters	2 liters
2 1/2 quarts	2.5 liters	2.5 liters
3 quarts	3 liters	3 liters
4 quarts	4 liters	4 liters

Weight

U.S. Units	Canadian Metric	Australian Metric
1 ounce	30 grams	30 grams
2 ounces	55 grams	60 grams
3 ounces	85 grams	90 grams
4 ounces (1/4 pound)	115 grams	125 grams
8 ounces (1/2 pound)	225 grams	225 grams
16 ounces (1 pound)	455 grams	500 grams
1 pound	455 grams	1/2 kilogram

Measurements

Inches	Centimeters
1	2.5
2	5.0
3	7.5
4	10.0
5	12.5
6	15.0
7	17.5
8	20.5
9	23.0
10	25.5
11	28.0
12	30.5
13	33.0

Temperatures

Fahrenheit	Celsius
32°	0°
212°	100°
250°	120°
275°	140°
300°	150°
325°	160°
350°	180°
375°	190°
400°	200°
425°	220°
450°	230°
475°	240°
500°	260°

Note: The recipes in this cookbook have not been developed or tested using metric measures. When converting recipes to metric, some variations in quality may be noted.

Helpful Nutrition and Cooking Information

Nutrition Guidelines

We provide nutrition information for each recipe that includes calories, fat, cholesterol, sodium, carbohydrate, fiber and protein. Individual food choices can be based on this information.

RECOMMENDED INTAKE FOR A DAILY DIET OF 2,000 CALORIES AS SET BY THE FOOD AND DRUG ADMINISTRATION

Total Fat	Less than 65g
Saturated Fat	Less than 20g
Cholesterol	Less than 300mg
Sodium	Less than 2,400mg
Total Carbohydrate	300g
Dietary Fiber	25g

Criteria Used for Calculating Nutrition Information

- The first ingredient was used wherever a choice is given (such as 1/3 cup sour cream or plain yogurt).
- The first ingredient amount was used wherever a range is given (such as 3- to 3-1/2–pound cut-up broiler-fryer chicken).
- The first serving number was used wherever a range is given (such as 4 to 6 servings).
- "If desired" ingredients and recipe variations were not included (such as sprinkle with brown sugar, if desired).
- Only the amount of a marinade or frying oil that is estimated to be absorbed by the food during preparation or cooking was calculated.

Ingredients Used in Recipe Testing and Nutrition Calculations

- Ingredients used for testing represent those that the majority of consumers use in their homes: large eggs, 2% milk, 80%-lean ground beef, canned ready-to-use chicken broth and vegetable oil spread containing not less than 65 percent fat.
- Fat-free, low-fat or low-sodium products were not used, unless otherwise indicated.
- Solid vegetable shortening (not butter, margarine, nonstick cooking sprays or vegetable oil spread, as they can cause sticking problems) was used to grease pans, unless otherwise indicated.

Equipment Used in Recipe Testing

We use equipment for testing that the majority of consumers use in their homes. If a specific piece of equipment (such as a wire whisk) is necessary for recipe success, it is listed in the recipe.

- Cookware and bakeware without nonstick coatings were used, unless otherwise indicated.
- No dark-colored, black or insulated bakeware was used.
- When a pan is specified in a recipe, a metal pan was used; a baking dish or pie plate means ovenproof glass was used.
- An electric hand mixer was used for mixing only when mixer speeds are specified in the recipe directions. When a mixer speed is not given, a spoon or fork was used.

Cooking Terms Glossary

Beat: Mix ingredients vigorously with spoon, fork, wire whisk, hand beater or electric mixer until smooth and uniform.

Boil: Heat liquid until bubbles rise continuously and break on the surface and steam is given off. For rolling boil, the bubbles form rapidly.

Chop: Cut into coarse or fine irregular pieces with a knife, food chopper, blender or food processor.

Cube: Cut into squares 1/2 inch or larger.

Dice: Cut into squares smaller than 1/2 inch.

Grate: Cut into tiny particles using small rough holes of grater (citrus peel or chocolate).

Grease: Rub the inside surface of a pan with shortening, using pastry brush, piece of waxed paper or paper towel, to prevent food from sticking during baking (as for some casseroles).

Julienne: Cut into thin, matchlike strips, using knife or food processor (vegetables, fruits, meats).

Mix: Combine ingredients in any way that distributes them evenly.

Sauté: Cook foods in hot oil or margarine over medium-high heat with frequent tossing and turning motion.

Shred: Cut into long thin pieces by rubbing food across the holes of a shredder, as for cheese, or by using a knife to slice very thinly, as for cabbage.

Simmer: Cook in liquid just below the boiling point on top of the stove; usually after reducing heat from a boil. Bubbles will rise slowly and break just below the surface.

Stir: Mix ingredients until uniform consistency. Stir once in a while for stirring occasionally, often for stirring frequently and continuously for stirring constantly.

Toss: Tumble ingredients (such as green salad) lightly with a lifting motion, usually to coat evenly or mix with another food.

INDEX

Complete your cookbook library with these *Betty Crocker* titles

Betty Crocker's Best Bread Machine Cookbook
Betty Crocker's Best Chicken Cookbook
Betty Crocker's Best Christmas Cookbook
Betty Crocker's Best of Baking
Betty Crocker's Best of Healthy and Hearty Cooking
Betty Crocker's Best-Loved Recipes
Betty Crocker's Bisquick® Cookbook
Betty Crocker Bisquick® II Cookbook
Betty Crocker Bisquick® Impossibly Easy Pies
Betty Crocker's Complete Thanksgiving Cookbook
Betty Crocker's Cook Book for Boys and Girls
Betty Crocker's Cook It Quick
Betty Crocker's Cookbook, 9th Edition—*The* **BIG RED** *Cookbook*®
Betty Crocker's Cookbook, Bridal Edition
Betty Crocker's Cookie Book
Betty Crocker's Cooking Basics
Betty Crocker's Cooking for Two
Betty Crocker's Cooky Book, Facsimile Edition
Betty Crocker's Diabetes Cookbook
Betty Crocker Easy Family Dinners with Rotisserie Chicken
Betty Crocker's Easy Slow Cooker Dinners
Betty Crocker's Eat and Lose Weight
Betty Crocker's Entertaining Basics
Betty Crocker's Flavors of Home
Betty Crocker 4-Ingredient Dinners
Betty Crocker's Great Grilling
Betty Crocker's Healthy New Choices
Betty Crocker's Indian Home Cooking
Betty Crocker's Italian Cooking
Betty Crocker's Kids Cook!
Betty Crocker's Kitchen Library
Betty Crocker's Living with Cancer Cookbook
Betty Crocker's Low-Fat Low-Cholesterol Cooking Today
Betty Crocker More Slow Cooker Recipes
Betty Crocker's New Cake Decorating
Betty Crocker's New Chinese Cookbook
Betty Crocker's A Passion for Pasta
Betty Crocker's Pasta Favorites
Betty Crocker's Picture Cook Book, Facsimile Edition
Betty Crocker's Quick & Easy Cookbook
Betty Crocker's Slow Cooker Cookbook
Betty Crocker's Ultimate Cake Mix Cookbook
Betty Crocker's Vegetarian Cooking